CHANGE

—YOUR—

WORLD

ALSO BY JOHN C. MAXWELL

CHANGE

—YOUR—

WORLD

HOW ANYONE, ANYWHERE CAN
MAKE A DIFFERENCE

JOHN C. MAXWELL
AND ROB HOSKINS

HARPERCOLLINS
LEADERSHIP

AN IMPRINT OF HARPERCOLLINS

Published by HarperCollins Leadership, an imprint of HarperCollins Focus LLC.

Published in association with Yates & Yates, www.yates2.com.

Scripture quotations marked NIV are from the Holy Bible, New International Version®, NIV®. Copyright © 1973, 1978, 1984, 2011 by Biblica, Inc.® Used by permission of Zondervan. All rights reserved worldwide. www.zondervan.com. The "NIV" and "New International Version" are trademarks registered in the United States Patent and Trademark Office by Biblica, Inc.®

Scripture quotations marked NLT are from the Holy Bible, New Living Translation. Copyright © 1996, 2004, 2015 by Tyndale House Foundation. Used by permission of Tyndale House Ministries, Carol Stream, Illinois 60188. All rights reserved.

Any internet addresses, phone numbers, or company or product information printed in this book are offered as a resource and are not intended in any way to be or to imply an endorsement by HarperCollins Leadership, nor does HarperCollins Leadership vouch for the existence, content, or services of these sites, phone numbers, companies, or products beyond the life of this book.

ISBN 978-1-4002-2492-0 (ITPE)
ISBN 978-1-4041-1572-9 (CU)

Library of Congress Cataloging-in-Publication Data
Names: Maxwell, John C., 1947–author. | Hoskins, Rob, author.
Title: Change your world: how anyone, anywhere can make a difference Description: Nashville: HarperCollins Leadership, 2020. | Includes
bibliographical references.
Identifiers: LCCN 2020022985 (print) | LCCN 2020022986 (ebook) | ISBN 9781400222315 (hardcover) | ISBN 9781400222322 (epub)
Subjects: LCSH: Change (Psychology) | Hope. | Goal (Psychology) | Social change. | Leadership.
Classification: LCC BF637.C4 .M379 2020 (print) | LCC BF637.C4 (ebook) | DDC 158—dc23
LC record available at https://lccn.loc.gov/2020022985
LC ebook record available at https://lccn.loc.gov/2020022986

Printed in the United States of America

21 22 23 24 25   LSC   10 9 8 7 6 5 4 3 2 1

John
Change Your World is dedicated to my Legacy Partners.
Their generosity and commitment to transformation
enable the vision to be a reality. The dream is free, but the
journey isn't. Thanks for being on the journey with me!
Love, JM

Rob
This book is dedicated to the love of my life Kim,
who knows me, knows what's best for us and has and
will always fiercely defend, creatively promote, and
wisely guide us towards our beautiful destiny.

CONTENTS

Acknowledgments

John:

I want to say thank you to all the members of my team who helped to make this book possible: Jason Brooks, Mark Cole, Linda Eggers, Carolyn Kokinda, Erin Miller, Charlie Wetzel, and Stephanie Wetzel. You all added incredible value to me and to this book. Thank you for helping me change our world!

Rob:

This book couldn't have been written without the thirty-plus year transformation journey that all my colleagues and OneHope team have been on; learning and discovering together. Particularly for this book, thank you David Branker, Chad Causey, Nicole Johansson, and Tena Stone for your extensive review, readings, and fantastic contributions. Jenna Scott, you are a champion and master writer, editor, researcher, and advisor. You are all as elite in your fields as you are humble; your contributions to this book are an investment in others to begin their journeys to change the world.

Authors' Note

The book you're reading was written by two people. Sometimes for readers that can be awkward. Or confusing. When you read a sentence or paragraph, who is the person communicating to you? Is it John Maxwell or Rob Hoskins?

Whenever two or more people collaborate in writing a book, they have to decide how they will communicate. Should we say that I (John) do this and I (Rob) do that? We've seen this kind of approach before in a cowritten book, where both people use "I" and put which is which in parentheses. We think that's really awkward.

Should we use two different fonts and ask you to keep track of who is who? We bet that would get old fast. You'd have to keep going back to the beginning of the book to keep track, assuming you could tell one font from the other. Another option would be to put our names before each paragraph in the book, such as in an interview. But we believe that would make for choppy reading.

If we were on stage, it would be easy. We both do a lot of speaking. If we were on a platform at a live event, you'd see our faces and hear our voices and know instantly who was saying what. We wish we could speak to you personally, but you know books don't work that way.

We want to make this reading experience enjoyable for you and as easy as possible, because this book is really about you and how you can change your world. So here's what you can expect. The voice you're hearing as you read this is John's. Rob has graciously allowed me to take the role of the older brother, doing the primary speaking. So, as you read, we hope it will feel like you are sitting with Rob and me conversing, but I'm doing most of the talking. You'll see a lot of "we," "Rob and I," and "Rob and me" in this book. But please know that Rob and I are equal partners in the thinking and writing of this book. What we share comes from our hearts, our dedication to changing our world to make it a better place, and our decades of experience of investing in others. Rob and I really want to help you. When you get to the end of the last chapter, we'll even offer you a way to take immediate steps for making a difference, if you're not already doing it on your own.

So settle in and enjoy the journey. We hope *Change Your World* will open your eyes, help you see your environment in a different way, change the way you live, and transform the world around you.

CHAPTER 1

WE CAN'T WAIT FOR CHANGE

Hope has two beautiful daughters; their names are Anger and Courage. Anger at the way things are, and Courage to see that they do not remain as they are.

—AUGUSTINE OF HIPPO

Rob and I are excited that you're reading these words, and we want to tell you something right off the top:

This book is written for you

IF

You want to change your world.

Going through the pages of this book, you will read about . . .

Missy, a volunteer at a school who was asked to share her apple, discovered hungry children, packed food into backpacks in her garage, and started a program that today feeds eighty-seven *thousand* kids.

Missy changed her world.

Bryan, who took his childhood trauma and pain and used it

I

build a safe place for sexually abused children so they could live with hope, dignity, and unconditional love.

Bryan is changing his world.

Ethan, a third-grader who put his hand over his heart and asked, "Do you ever feel deep down here that you want to help make a difference?"

Ethan is only just beginning to change his world.

This book is written for you

IF

You want to change yourself.

You will be changed as you read about . . .

Charlee, a high school dropout with no sense of purpose in her life, who spent five months working with children in the slums of Africa and said, "I came home a totally, radically changed person."

Charlee was changed and now she is changing her world.

Rene, a man in Mexico who searched for his brother's murderer for ten years so he could exact revenge, but learned the value of forgiveness at transformation tables, chose to forgive the man, and changed his family's history.

Rene was changed and his life is getting better.

Yomila, a timid young woman from Guatemala who gained the courage and confidence to take a better job when she adopted a more positive attitude and now helps others in the villages surrounding her home.

Yomila has changed and is now helping others.

This book is written for you

IF

You want to be part of a transformational movement.

You will be inspired as you learn about . . .

Sam, the owner of a company that makes outdoor furniture who started making plastic face shields for medical workers braving the COVID-19 pandemic and brought together the people in his small community while making a difference.

Sam helped others create a movement in his town.

Cerro Porteño, one of Paraguay's most popular professional soccer teams, joined hands with rival Club Olimpia to teach good values to players at every level of their organization, and it's spreading to other teams and changing players' lives.

One team helped another and started a movement in their community.

Roy, who learned his son wanted to take his life because he was being bullied. While helping his son, Roy realized other parents and kids needed help, so he started an organization that now helps millions of kids in forty-two states.

Roy is part of a movement that is changing the country.

You have the potential to make a difference by joining with us as we help others or by starting a movement of your own.

You can change your world.

Rob and I have invested our lives in bringing positive change into the lives of people. This book has been written to encourage and equip you to be a catalyst for transformation in your world: your family, your workplace, your community. If you are already changing your world, we hope to help you become even better at it. If you are not yet involved in making a positive difference in the lives of others, we hope to encourage you to get started, and we want to teach you how to intentionally add value to people, because anyone, anywhere can make a difference.

Changing the world happens one life at a time. We are committed to helping people like you become a light of hope within your community. Thousands of volunteers have already become part of our transformation efforts, helping others to learn and live good values. (You can go to ChangeYourWorld.com to check that out.) In many countries around the world, they are making a difference through the eight streams of influence: government, education, business, religion, media, arts, sports, and healthcare. Rob and I envision a day when people from every background, in every country are adding value to people, making a difference, and changing their world. That day will become a reality when you and others like you commit to it.

WHAT NEEDS TO CHANGE?

Looking at our world, it's pretty easy to see that things could change for the better. Wouldn't it be wonderful to have better schools? Better neighborhoods? More positive workplaces? Would you like to have a more connected family? Communities where people get along and work together for everyone's good? Wouldn't the world be better if people were more respectful, unified, and positive?

You probably know intuitively much of what can be read in newspaper headlines. We have reasons to believe our world needs to become better:

- Families are breaking down in the United States; where 9 percent of households in 1960 were led by single parents, in 2014 that number grew to 26 percent.[1]
- In 2014 about 2.5 million children experienced homelessness in the United States.[2]
- Civic engagement and volunteerism, two characteristics

4

that were once identified as America's strengths, have fallen drastically in the last fifty years.[3]

- In 2015 3.3 million people were victims of violent crime in the United States.[4]
- An estimate by the Institute for Economics and Peace recently concluded that violence costs the global economy $13.6 trillion a year.[5]
- Mental health issues are on the rise[6] and getting worse.[7]
- Corruption is a problem around the globe.[8]
- It's estimated that 40 million people worldwide are victims of modern slavery.[9]

We could go on, but we don't need to. Problems that could use our help are everywhere. We're betting you see things around you every day that you wish were better than they are.

But don't let that discourage or intimidate you. Did you know that positive changes are possible? Even huge ones? While we were working on this book, Rob shared some information with me that really surprised me. In 2013, a survey asking about extreme poverty—living on less than $1.90 a day—posed this question: "In the last 30 years, has the proportion of the world population living in extreme poverty increased, stayed the same, or decreased?" Here are the answers people gave to the question:

- 55% said extreme poverty had increased
- 33% said it had stayed the same
- 12% said it had decreased[10]

What's your guess? I was shocked and pleased to learn that extreme poverty rates worldwide have actually *decreased*.

Dramatically! Look at this graph to see how extreme poverty rates have steadily gone down since 1800 and notice how they have *plunged* since the 1950s.

EXTREME POVERTY RATE FROM 1800 TO TODAY

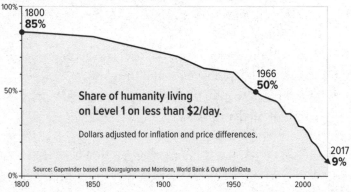

And the extreme poverty rate continues to go down. That's great news, yet we rarely hear anything about it. In 2018 the Brookings Institute reported,

> Something of enormous global significance is happening almost without notice. For the first time since agriculture-based civilization began 10,000 years ago, the majority of humankind is no longer poor or vulnerable to falling into poverty. By our calculations, as of this month, just over 50 percent of the world's population, or some 3.8 billion people, live in households with enough discretionary expenditure to be considered "middle class" or "rich." About the same number of people are living in households that are poor or vulnerable to poverty. So September 2018 marks a global tipping point. After this, for the first time

ever, the poor and vulnerable will no longer be a majority in the world. Barring some unfortunate global economic setback, this marks the start of a new era of a middle-class majority.[11]

This is great news that should give us great hope. We believe if extreme poverty can be changed—something that has been a problem for all of human history—so can other problems, great and small. The world can change for the better. People like you and like us can be difference makers.

Somebody Do Something!

If change is possible, why aren't we doing more to change our world? The Chinese philosopher Lao Tzu said, "If we don't change the direction we're going, we are likely to end up where we are headed." The reality is that most of us are waiting for somebody else to do something about the problems we see. We want change, but we hope that some*one* some*where* will do some*thing* to bring it about.

- We wait for the **government** to do something.
- We want the **health care** system to do something.
- We believe **education** will do something.
- We look to **business** to do something.
- We imagine **media** will do something.
- We wish **arts and entertainment** would do something.
- We think **sports** will do something.
- We hope **religious institutions** will do something.

But the fact is that we can't wait for change. While the influencers and institutions we listed above are all beneficial, the rest of us can't be passive bystanders. If we want the world to be a better place and we hope for conditions of need in the world to improve, then we need to change. We need to take action.

> "IF WE DON'T CHANGE THE DIRECTION WE'RE GOING, WE ARE LIKELY TO END UP WHERE WE ARE HEADED."
> —LAO TZU

Rob and I have spent our lives helping people and leading organizations whose purpose is to add value to people. We've traveled the world and interacted with people from every continent and from more cultures than we can count. And we are convinced of one thing: **transformation is possible for anyone willing to learn and live good values, value people, and collaborate with others to create a positive values culture.** That means *you* can change your world. You don't have to be rich. You don't have to be famous. You don't have to move to another country. You don't need an education. You don't need an organization. And you certainly don't need someone else's permission. You need to give *yourself* permission. You can transform yourself and the world around you. As Mahatma Gandhi said, "In a gentle way you can shake the world." But for that to happen, you need to change.

FIRST, CHANGE YOUR THINKING

I recently read *The Art of Possibility* by Rosamund Stone Zander and Benjamin Zander. They referred to an old puzzle I was familiar with, the nine dots on a page. In fact, I used it as an illustration in my book *Developing the Leader Within You*. But they examined it in a new way, which I believe is helpful here for illustrating the importance of changing how we think. First, we want to acquaint you with the puzzle. Here's the challenge: find a way to connect all nine dots below using four straight lines *without* lifting your pen or pencil from the paper. If you've never seen this before, give it a try.

     ●   ●   ●

     ●   ●   ●

     ●   ●   ●

Were you able to do it? Most people have a hard time figuring out how to make it work. Why? Because they think inside the box. But the only way to solve the problem is to change the way you think and get outside of a self-imposed way of thinking. The Zanders wrote,

> The frames our minds create define—and *con*fine—what we perceive to be possible. Every problem, every dilemma, every dead end we find ourselves facing in life, only appears unsolvable inside a particular frame or point of view. Enlarge the box, or create another frame around the data, and the problems vanish, while new opportunities appear.

If you *think* you can't change the world, your assumptions are putting you in a box. The Zanders explained that the assumptions we make often restrict our thinking and therefore restrict our possibilities. But they also tell how we can change:

> You can shift the framework [of your beliefs and thinking] to one whose underlying assumptions allow for the conditions you desire. Let your thoughts and actions spring from a new framework and see what happens.[12]

THE ASSUMPTIONS WE MAKE OFTEN RESTRICT OUR THINKING AND THEREFORE RESTRICT OUR POSSIBILITIES.

If you still don't know the solution to the puzzle with the dots, here it is. You have to draw outside the lines you may have arbitrarily imposed surrounding the dots. You have to change the way you think.

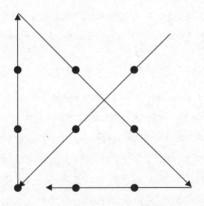

Gandhi said, "For things to change, first I must change." Changing your world requires a similar shift in thinking. You need to challenge your assumptions—from assuming you *can't* or *shouldn't* try to change your world to someone who *can* and *should*. You need to *believe* you can do something about the problems you see. You need to believe you can make a difference no matter who you are, where you are, and with whatever you have. You need to have hope.

Then, Harness Your Hope

You cannot overestimate the importance of real, active hope for changing the world. Jonathan Sacks, in *The Dignity of Difference*, wrote, "One of the most important distinctions I have learned in the course of reflection on Jewish history is the difference between optimism and hope. Optimism is the belief that things will be better. Hope is the faith that, together, we can make things better. Optimism is a passive virtue; hope, an active one. It takes no courage to be an optimist, but it takes a great deal of courage to have hope."[13] Most people would agree that optimism is greater than pessimism, but it's a fantastic thought that hope is greater than optimism.

> "Optimism is the belief that things will be better. Hope is the faith that, together, we can make things better."
> —Jonathan Sacks

We want to invite you to move up to that higher level of thinking, more elevated than pessimism or optimism. We invite you to become a person of hope. We want to help you become someone who possesses a healthy amount of positive discontent, believes the world can change, and knows you can be an important part of that change. We encourage you to . . .

HAVE HOPE FOR YOURSELF

Belief in yourself is a powerful thing. Psychologist Ellen J. Langer wrote about a study she conducted that showed the impact of belief.

> We explored the mindset most of us have regarding the excellent vision air force pilots have. All participants were given a vision test. One group of participants was then encouraged to role-play "air force pilots." They dressed the part and, in uniform, sat in a flight simulator. They were asked to read the letters on the wing of a nearby plane, which were actually part of an eye chart. Those participants who adopted the "pilot" mindset, primed to have excellent vision, showed improved vision over those who were . . . simply asked to read an eye chart from the same distance.[14]

We want you to adopt a change-my-world mindset. You have much greater control over your ability to accomplish difficult things than you might believe, but you must have hope and believe in yourself.

Do you know what convinces me that you should believe in yourself, have hope for yourself, and be certain you can change for the better? Because I've personally experienced changing for the better. I'm known as a leadership expert, but the most difficult person I've ever had to lead is myself. Thankfully, I've grown. I've gotten better in my ability to do what I should do, when I should do it, with the right motives for doing it.

People can change. Over the years I've discovered that people change when one or more things happen:

People Change When They Hurt
Enough That They Have To

The most basic impetus for change is pain. From the time we are first able to make choices as a child, we instinctively avoid pain. But a better response to pain is to change so we are no longer hurt by it. Our hope is this book will give you a positive pathway forward and provide hope if you're hurting.

People Change When They See Enough
That They Are Inspired To

Early in my career I was inspired when I saw that developing people as leaders has such a positive impact. The discovery that everything rises and falls on leadership changed the way I thought, worked, and interacted with others.

Perhaps you've been affected by something that has inspired you. If so, that's fantastic. If not, as you read this book, you will become acquainted with the stories of people who saw a better life or more excellent future for those around them and who took action to catalyze change. Please allow their example to move you and open your eyes to the need that maybe only you can address.

People Change When They Learn
Enough That They Want To

When you believe there's nothing you can do about a problem, it's disheartening and demotivating. But when you begin to learn how you can take steps to start making a difference, it will propel you to take action.

Rob and I believe you already have the desire and ability to be an agent for change. Maybe you're already making a difference and want to expand your impact. Whether that's true or you have yet to get started, this book will give you a simple, straightforward game plan to take the steps needed to incite positive change.

People Change When They Receive Enough That They Are Able To

The world is not looking for more dreamers. It is looking for dream makers. Brad Montague, the creator of the *Kid President* videos and television show, stated it clearly:

> Dare to Dream, but please also Do.
> For Dreamers are many, but Doers are few.[15]

As you read through this book and put what you learn into practice by taking action, you will start to see changes in yourself and the people whose lives you touch, and you will help others to make their dreams come true.

That's what Bryan Jarrett has done—helped others' dreams come true by giving them what they need to change. Jarrett grew up in an unstable home situation in a small, rural farming community in the South. His father would often disappear for days or weeks at a time, until one day he never returned. Without the protection of his father's presence, Jarrett became a victim of repeated sexual abuse from an extended family member. He started drinking in his teens to cope with the abuse and to numb the sense of abandonment he felt.[16]

Eventually Jarrett became a person of faith and began to heal. He immediately wanted to help others, particularly the overlooked, the less fortunate, and the underdog. When he first started, almost thirty years ago, he did a lot of youth work. "As I began to heal, I began to feel the freedom to talk about it," he said, speaking about the childhood sexual abuse he suffered. "I say this all the time: rodents and roaches play in the dark, and when the lights come on, they all go find a place to hide.

> "DARE TO DREAM, BUT PLEASE ALSO DO. FOR DREAMERS ARE MANY, BUT DOERS ARE FEW."
> —BRAD MONTAGUE

"There was freedom for me in being able to talk about it," said Jarrett. "As I shared my story, I realized that thousands of kids across this country were connecting with my story, and then I started looking into the numbers of people who admit to being sexually abused."[17]

His heart stirred, and he decided he needed to do something about it. Jarrett and his wife established Lonesome Dove Ranch to help children who had suffered abuse begin to heal. Most of the kids they serve are in foster care.

"I didn't start out to engage kids in the foster system, but identifying children who have dealt with sexual abuse is hard outside of the foster system," said Jarrett. "A lot of the kids in the foster system are there because of some level of abuse, much of it sexual abuse. We founded Lonesome Dove Ranch in 2015 to serve the needs of children who have been exploited and sexually abused. It was born out of my own pain."[18]

Each week the ranch hosts fifty children who are served by 150 adults, nearly all of whom are volunteers. "The needs—emotionally, mentally, sometimes physically—are extreme."[19] Volunteers at the ranch help the kids and serve them freely. "We give the kids dignity and love without wanting anything back," said Jarrett. "Most of these kids have only been shown love because there was an agenda. We have no agenda."[20]

Giving each child individual time and attention enables healing to begin within a week. The ranch's success with children has made it possible for them to open additional camps, so they now have five different locations.

Jarrett took the hurt he felt, the vision he saw, and the lessons he learned and used them to have hope in himself to make a difference. Then he asked others to join him, and with what he received, he had the courage to bring Lonesome Dove Ranch into existence. He is changing his world one child at a time. "When your past, your pain and your passion overlap," said Jarrett, "you find the sweet spot of your purpose in life."[21]

You can find your sweet spot too. You can be the change you want to see in the world. It all starts with changing yourself. As our friend Tony Evans said, "If you want a better world, composed of better nations, inhabited by better states, filled with better counties, made up of better cities, comprised of better neighborhoods, illuminated by better churches, populated by better families, then you have to start by becoming a better person." The first step in that process is having hope that you can.

HAVE HOPE FOR OTHERS

The changes you make within yourself will give you the confidence and credibility and hope to help others. You can become what we call a "hope helper." It requires you to be positive and to focus on the positive change you can create, not the negative situation you want to eliminate. Hope can move us toward something better and bring others with us.

We like the positive approach to change that the nonprofit, philanthropic Chandler Foundation takes to making a difference. They believe that instead of focusing on fixing poverty, we should instead build and promote prosperity. How? They say transformation occurs both top-down and bottom-up. From the top, leaders must possess good character and earn trust from their people. They write, "Countries with high-trust cultures—those where regulations and laws are fair and enforced, with secure and stable business environments, and with trustworthy leaders—attract capital and investment, which drive economic growth and employment." From the bottom, people's dreams, beliefs, core values, and skills empower them to climb the social mobility ladder into the middle class, which they term the engine room of greater prosperity.[22]

Clayton M. Christensen, Efosa Ojomo, and Karen Dillon, in their book *The Prosperity Paradox*, agree. They stated, "It may sound counterintuitive . . . [but] enduring prosperity for many countries will not come from fixing poverty. It will come from investing in innovations that create new markets within these countries."[23]

The negatives in life may attract our attention and open our eyes to the need for change, but only by being positive and by helping to create and offer a better way can we positively change our world. Creating positive change in communities is similar to developing people. Good leaders focus on people's strengths and help them to develop those strengths. They don't focus on their weaknesses. Similarly, to help others live a better life, you don't focus on their problems. You focus on positive solutions that provide a better way for them to live.

HAVE HOPE FOR A BETTER FUTURE

Journalist Linda Ellerbee said, "What I like most about change is that it can be a synonym for 'hope.' If you are taking a risk, what you are really saying is, 'I believe in tomorrow, and I will be part of it.'"[24]

That's what Ruslan Maliuta did in Ukraine. Because Ruslan spoke English, he was asked to do some translation work for an American couple who had come to Kiev to adopt a child. When the adoption went through, Ruslan witnessed the joy of this couple connecting with their new daughter. Ruslan recalled, "It was like they already belonged together. They just fit—like something they had lost had been found." That experience made a mark on him.

> "WHAT I LIKE MOST ABOUT CHANGE IS THAT IT CAN BE A SYNONYM FOR 'HOPE.'"
> —LINDA ELLERBEE

Dale Carnegie said, "Most of the things in the world have been accomplished by people who have kept on trying when there seemed to be no hope at all." That was the situation in Ukraine at the time. There were perhaps as many as one hundred thousand orphans in the country, many of whom lived on the streets. Ruslan began working with an organization that rescued abandoned, neglected, and abused children. Because his heart went out to these orphaned children, he began working to find families and homes for them. And he began to dream of a better future for them and for his country. He wondered, "What if Ukraine could become a country that no longer had orphans?"

Ruslan began working with a group of friends to create the better future he hoped for. As their work began to succeed, people from other countries asked his advice, and his vision grew. That made him want to help orphans, not just in Ukraine, but around the world. It's estimated there are currently anywhere from two to eight million children living in orphanages around the world.[25] Ruslan's desire to change his world, fueled by hope for a better future, led him to start World Without Orphans, a network of people who work to place orphans in families, not institutions. "The vision is really for every child to grow up in a loving, caring, safe family," said Ruslan. Currently the movement has launched initiatives in thirty-eight countries, with an additional forty-seven nations they are working with for future partnerships."[26] They have hope for a better future, and that keeps them working to make a difference.

Hope Fuels Urgency

When you've harnessed a strong sense of hope, what should you do with it? Too often, even if we believe we should do something, we don't. And it's not that we tell ourselves, "I'll never do that." Instead, we say to ourselves, "I'll do it tomorrow." But then we get too busy or too distracted to follow through. And if we *do* remember, we think, "Oh, I don't have enough time today. I'll do it tomorrow." And we miss the opportunity again.

How can we fix that? By infusing our hope with a sense of urgency. If you think about it, the phrase *we can't wait for change* can be read two ways. The first meaning is that we shouldn't hold back, expecting someone else to start making the changes we want to see. But there's a second way to read that phrase, the way a child would say, "I can't wait for Christmas!" It's a sense of anticipation, excitement, and urgency. That second meaning is what we need to adopt. And each of us needs to make it personal, from "*We* can't wait for change" to "*I* can't wait for change." That sense of urgency can propel us to action.

Here are some of our observations about how urgency works and what it does for us.

URGENCY STARTS WITHIN

If people resistant to change had a theme song, it would be the old hymn that says, "I shall not be, I shall not be moved." But for people who want to change their world, they'd rather be singing, "I shall not be stopped!"

Business consultant Rob Llewellyn observed,

> Have you noticed that the people who make things happen in this world value and share a similar sense of urgency?
>
> Regardless of what people aim to achieve, whether in sport, business or otherwise, those who set themselves apart from the rest maintain a sense of urgency in order to be the best they can be. They choose not to disconnect from what they are aiming to achieve, and they pursue it—regardless of what anyone else thinks or says—because their sense of urgency is an integral part of who they are.[27]

Change begins on the inside. We need to tap into our desire to see change happen and enable it to strengthen into a sense of urgency. Then we need to sustain that sense of urgency. As Ralph Marston, author of *The Daily Motivator*, said, "Success requires both urgency and patience. Be urgent about making the effort, and patient about seeing the results."

URGENCY FEEDS DESIRE

When you harness your hope and tap into a sense of urgency for change, it only increases your desire to see that change come about. You could call it a kind of positive, healthy discontent. But without that urgency, you lose momentum and energy. We agree with motivational speaker Jim Rohn, who said, "Without a sense of urgency, a desire loses its value."

There's a story that's been around for a long time and has appeared all

> "SUCCESS REQUIRES BOTH URGENCY AND PATIENCE. BE URGENT ABOUT MAKING THE EFFORT, AND PATIENT ABOUT SEEING THE RESULTS."
> —RALPH MARSTON

over the internet in various forms, including poetry. The original inspiration for it was a real-life anecdote told by Loren Eiseley in *The Unexpected Universe*.[28] The gist of the story is that a man walks along the beach one morning after a storm has washed thousands of starfish ashore. As the man walks, he sees a boy at a distance stooping down and doing something. When he gets closer, the man realizes that the boy is picking up starfish, one by one, and throwing them back into the water.

Surprised by the boy's action, the man says to him, "There are thousands of starfish stranded as far as the eye can see. What possible difference can it make?"

The boy holds up a starfish he just picked up and looks at it for a moment. Then he tosses it into the sea and replies, "It makes a difference for this one."

I mentioned to my friend Traci Morrow that we were telling the starfish story in this book, and she told me how it impacted her in a deeply personal way. Traci said that she had known since she was a teenager that she wanted to adopt children someday, and even before she married her husband, K. C., they talked about adopting and agreed that, when the time came, they would. After they married, they had four biological children in five years, so life was really busy. But a day came when their oldest child was thirteen, and they believed it was time. Their plan was to adopt two boys from Ethiopia. However, as they were going through the process, they learned there were 4.5 *million* orphans in Ethiopia. That information overwhelmed them so much so that they wondered, *Should we try to adopt more kids? Would adopting these two boys make any difference at all?*

> THE PEOPLE WHO CHANGE THE WORLD ARE THOSE WHO *WANT* TO AND DON'T *WAIT* TO.

They were paralyzed, but then some friends shared the starfish story with them, and it change their thinking. "The starfish story really helped us to come to grips with the fact that while we weren't making a significant dent in the orphan crisis in Ethiopia, it made a significant difference for our two boys' lives," said Traci. And then she told me, "To this day, we have two starfish hanging in our home to remind us that doing whatever we can really matters."

Rob and I admire Traci and every other person like her who is willing to take action to make a difference, regardless of how small their efforts might feel at the time. The people who change the world are those who *want* to and don't *wait* to. Ralph Waldo Emerson said, "That which we persist in doing becomes easier for us to do; not because the nature of the thing itself has changed, but that our power to do is increased."

URGENCY INSPIRES COURAGE

Yesterday is not ours to recover, but tomorrow is ours to win or lose. It takes courage to believe the best is yet to come. That courageous faith will help us to win tomorrow. But we find it when we allow ourselves to feel the urgency of today.

In *Dare to Lead*, Brené Brown shares an interesting discovery she made after talking to a large, diverse group of top leaders:

> We started our interviews with senior leaders with one question: *What, if anything, about the way people are leading today needs to change in order for leaders to be successful in a complex, rapidly changing environment where we're faced with seemingly intractable challenges and an insatiable demand for innovation?*
>
> There was one answer across the interviews: **We need braver leaders and more courageous cultures.**[29]

Leadership is influence—nothing more, nothing less. So if you influence just one other person, you are a leader. When you add courage to your leadership, then you create opportunities for change, which in turn changes culture.

URGENCY CALLS FOR ACTION

Malcolm Gladwell said in a presentation on his book *David and Goliath*, "The most successful entrepreneurs not only have courage and imagination, they also have a sense of urgency. They're not willing to wait. They have a burning desire to get something done."[30] What he says of business entrepreneurs can be said of people who create transformation. They don't want to wait. They want to get something done. The feeling of urgency moves them to take *action*. Right now!

Recently I visited a school that my friend, entrepreneur Casey Crawford, founded in an at-risk community. While I was there, I visited a group of third-graders, and a boy named Ethan asked, "Do you ever feel, deep down here [pointing to his heart], that you want to help people and make a difference?" I couldn't believe it. I looked to see if anyone on my team had prompted him to ask this question, but it was clear the question was genuine.

"Ethan, that's *exactly* the way I feel," I answered. "Every day, deep down in my heart, I want to make a difference." Then I gave Ethan a hug and said, "You are going to change your world."

> IT DOESN'T MATTER HOW OLD YOU ARE. IT DOESN'T MATTER WHAT YOU HAVE OR HAVEN'T DONE YET. IT'S NEVER TOO LATE TO DO SOMETHING TO CHANGE YOUR WORLD.

Do you feel like Ethan? Do you feel the desire deep down in your heart to make a positive difference in the lives of others? It doesn't matter how old you are. It doesn't matter what you have or haven't done yet. It's never too late to do something to change your world. A Turkish proverb says, "No matter how far you have gone on a wrong road, turn back." You can turn in a new direction right now and do something to change your world.

A RIGHT WRONG TURN

Rob was recently turned in a new direction and developed a strong sense of urgency for changing part of his world as he was driving to his office in Pompano Beach, Florida. He waited as usual at a red light just a few blocks from work. He normally turned left to go into his office park, but for some reason, on this day, he felt compelled to make a right turn onto a road he'd never traveled before. It took him into a small urban community called Avondale.

As Rob drove around, what he saw arrested his attention. He witnessed a drug deal, prostitutes soliciting customers in the middle of the day, gang members holding court with school-aged boys who should have been in class, and moms clearly under the influence watching passively as bunches of children ran around on their lawns. What he viewed in that two-block radius—practically across the street from his office—mirrored conditions he had seen in some of the most at-risk slums he had visited in places like Dharavi in Mumbai, India; Comas in Lima, Peru; and Kibera in Nairobi, Kenya.

"I felt angry," Rob said. "I was angry at the condition of my community. Right across the street from my work were people suffering, trapped by their circumstances. I felt the pain of those fathers, unable to provide for their kids. I was angry at the waste of human potential. Angry because I knew these children, through no fault of their own, were trapped in a societal prison of poverty, abuse, and neglect. But I was also angry at myself, angry that I hadn't seen what was happening right in front of me. It deeply convicted me that although I was helping kids around the world, I had failed to see that hopelessness lived next door to me."

Rob pulled to the side of the road and cried.

"Tears were flowing down my cheeks, but from deep in my heart, courage began to rise out of my anger," he said. "I began to see possibilities, how tangible, substantive, and lasting changes could come to my neighbors in Avondale."

Rob was determined to do something. How could he, the leader of OneHope, not help his actual neighbors when he leads an organization that impacts children in nearly every country around the world and has offered hope to over a billion children, many in the most hopeless and hard-to-reach places on the planet? He had brought together people to help alleviate poverty, stop injustice, and prevent teenage pregnancy, suicide, and addiction around the globe. He knew he could do something to help with the problems he had just seen, and his sense of anger and conviction stoked his sense of urgency.

Rob drove out of Avondale, and as soon as he stepped foot in his office, he started telling his team what he'd seen that morning. Because serving children and youth is what OneHope does, these tremendous needs immediately resonated with everyone. They got to work researching Avondale, calling people who could help, and building a plan to help make positive changes.

Their research revealed the community consisted of about three thousand people in nine hundred residences. The area would be termed "struggling urban diversity," according to the U.S. Census. The people who lived in Avondale were mostly from broken families with a single parent, and they were living in poverty. The public schools in the area had earned a grade of F. Crime was beyond high. In fact, Avondale ranked in the bottom 1 percent of U.S. neighborhoods for safety, with 776 crimes per square mile per year, in contrast to the rest of Florida's average of 91 per square mile and the U.S. average of 50 per square mile. People in Avondale had a one in forty-four chance of being victims of crime and a 15 percent chance of being a victim of violent crime, more than eight times the national average! Gang rivalries were also creating a lot of the conflict in the area.

Despite the danger, Rob's team learned more by going door-to-door and talking to Avondale's residents, asking them about their lives, listening to their concerns, and finding out what they needed. The number-one answer was jobs, followed by role models for their children and English classes.

Rob knew that to help break the cycle of poverty in these families, they would have to "go young." Future success for people in poverty is tied to high school graduation.[31] But you can't start by focusing on helping kids in high school. You need to start when they're younger. What's the number-one determinant of whether kids graduate from high school? Third-grade literacy.[32] Along with other interventions, the most significant and powerful way to bring generational change to this community would be through good education, especially of younger kids with reading.

Rob and his team committed to serving the people of Avondale, which required some hard asks of themselves as well as enlisting the help of local organizations. "Avondale changed us dramatically as an organization," Rob told me. "OneHope became so dedicated to helping this community that we forfeited the for-profit space we had in our building and donated it to become a charter school and private academy for families in Avondale and the surrounding communities." All but 7 percent of the kids attending the school fall below the poverty line, but within the walls they have found a place of hope and love, and they are receiving an excellent education.

In addition to founding the school and after-school reading programs, OneHope also reached out to help adults. They organized classes in English as a second language, hosted health fairs, taught interviewing skills to job seekers, helped feed families in need, and provided mentors to help people grow.

Their collective efforts have made such a positive impact that crime in the area has gone down from 776 incidents per square mile to the 200s. Relationships between residents are improving, and the people of Avondale have hope for a better future. Not only is there widespread change in the neighborhood, but one of the students, whom we'll call Haylee, found hope and healing in a desperate situation. She was being raised by her grandmother because her mother was a drug addict and her father was in jail.

Working multiple jobs and trying to do the best she could for her granddaughter, Haylee's grandmother enrolled her in the new charter school. It has become a safe, secure place for her, and Haylee has been growing and thriving. But then last year, Haylee's grandma received a call that the girl's mom had passed away from a drug overdose. It's traumatic for a child to lose a parent and even harder when it is to drug addiction. However, Haylee is going to be okay because she is in a place filled with love and support.

A friend of the school who offers free counseling to any kids who need it has been doing grief counseling with Haylee. When Haylee shared with the counselor that she wanted a punching bag and gloves to help her work through her intense feelings, someone in the school community made sure Haylee received those items. Word also got out about the death of Haylee's mom, and complete strangers raised money to give to Haylee's grandma for her care. While the money won't fix all the problems they face, it will definitely alleviate some stressors during a hard time.

"When I think about Haylee or look at her face," Rob said, "my mind races back to that morning several years ago. I can't help but wonder if she was one of the children I saw on the street. What if I hadn't taken that right turn?"

Or what if he had chosen to do nothing? Would his inaction

have doomed her and her neighborhood to an existence of illiteracy, poverty, and hopelessness? Instead, he sees a young lady, not immune to the real-life struggles that face her and her grandma, but with a sparkle in her eye. She has a hope, assurance, and confidence born out of the loving, transformational investments made by people who care and believe that change is possible.

"My life turned around the day I drove through Avondale," Rob said. "I couldn't un-see what I had seen, and no excuse could have been compelling enough to allow me to drive along my merry way. My first thought was, *I must do something to help others!* Soon I began to discover that the change I wanted for them begin to change me. I learned that helping others, helped me!"

MAKE THE RIGHT TURN

As you read Rob's story, you might have said to yourself, *I'm not sure I can do anything like that. It seems so overwhelming. Where would I start? What would I do? I'm just one person. Could I really change my world?*

Rob and I are here to wholeheartedly tell you, "Yes, you can!" You can make a positive difference. Because you want to see change happen, and you want to live in a better world, you *can* make an impact. Everyone has plenty of reasons *not* to do something about the problems they see. Those are called excuses. A wise coach once told me, "Excuses are like armpits. Everyone has them and they all stink." The reality is that we can make excuses or we can make changes, *but we can't do both.*

When I was a kid, one of the cartoons I used to watch was *Popeye the Sailor.* The main character, Popeye, wore a sailor suit and had huge forearms with anchors tattooed on them. The mild-mannered Popeye always seemed to be trying to stop Bluto, a big bully, from stealing his girlfriend, Olive Oyl. At some point in every cartoon, Popeye would reach a point of frustration and say, "That's all I can stands, and I can't stands no more." He'd open a can of spinach, suck down the contents to gain superhuman strength, pummel the bully, and rescue his girl.

> WE CAN MAKE EXCUSES OR WE CAN MAKE CHANGES, *BUT WE CAN'T DO BOTH.*

Popeye's solution was eating a can of spinach. Our solution is making a commitment to change. Do you see a need for positive change somewhere around you? Are you willing to learn and live good values? Are you willing to value people? Are you willing to help others, add value to them, and invite them to experience the positive impact of good values and good choices? If you answer yes to those simple questions, then you can change your world. Hope is not far away. Change is in your hands. Don't allow anything to deter you. You can become a catalyst for change. In the next chapter, Rob and I will show you how to do that.

CHAPTER 2

BECOME A CATALYST FOR CHANGE

The people who are crazy enough to think
they can change the world are usually the
ones who do.

—STEVE JOBS

What does it mean to be a catalyst for change? The most common definition of the word comes from chemistry, where a catalyst is a substance that causes or speeds up a chemical reaction. But when Rob and I use the word *catalyst*, we're describing a person who creates positive change in their world through their ideas, actions, and influence.

When it comes to making a positive difference in the world, change occurs only when someone, somewhere takes responsibility for changing himself or herself and takes action to help others change too. Without the actions of some person, change doesn't happen.

FARM BOY WITH A HEART TO HELP

We often think of changing the world as something big that takes big plans, large teams, and huge resources. We overestimate the importance of big events and underestimate the value of small actions taken to help others. Some of the greatest catalysts for change in the world took small steps that seemed insignificant at the time—without fanfare, recognition, or reward—and simply allowed one step to lead to the next, ultimately leading to great change.

A fantastic example of that is Norman Borlaug. When Rob speaks to people about change, he sometimes asks his audience to name the most important person of the twentieth century. I don't know what your answer to that question would be, but Rob's is Borlaug.

Born in 1914, Norman Borlaug grew up working hard on the family farm in Iowa. His grandfather encouraged him to continue his education after high school,[1] so he pursued a degree in forestry at the University of Minnesota. At one point he had to leave school to work and earn money to complete his degree. His coworkers were poor and, he realized, starving. When he saw the positive impact it had when they were able to get food, he never forgot it. Borlaug said, "I saw how food changed them. . . . All of this left scars on me."[2] It also inspired him to continue his education, eventually earning graduate degrees in plant pathology.

After graduating in 1942 in the midst of World War II, he worked for two years on chemical compounds for DuPont to help with the country's war effort. But his desire to help starving people never left him. He joined the Rockefeller Foundation's Mexican hunger project so he could help countries like Mexico that were having trouble producing enough crops to feed their people.[3]

Borlaug spent countless hours, day after day, in the fields, crossing different strains of wheat to develop plants that could produce more. The work was hard and for decades went unrecognized.

In addition to his personal experience with food shortages, Borlaug had additional motivation. In the late 1940s, ecologist William Vogt wrote a book titled *Road to Survival* in which he warned that the human race was dangerously close to exhausting its resources.[4] By the late 1960s, when the earth's population exceeded three billion people, some scientists said food shortages due to overpopulation would be inevitable. Paul R. Ehrlich, a Stanford University biologist, wrote *The Population Bomb,* whose opening words were, "The battle to feed all of humanity is over," meaning it had already failed. He predicted that hundreds of millions of people would starve to death in the 1970s, including sixty-five million Americans. He believed India was doomed and that "England will not exist in the year 2000." He was convinced humanity was on the brink of "an utter breakdown of the capacity of the planet to support humanity."[5]

While Ehrlich and others pointed out problems and predicted catastrophe, *Borlaug worked.* He took the action he could: he used his knowledge of plants and his passion for change and helped to create strains of wheat that could produce more. After years of quiet work, he developed a variety of wheat that tripled or quadrupled wheat production on the same plot of land. By the early 1960s many farms in Mexico were using Borlaug's innovations, and wheat production had increased sixfold compared to the early 1940s when he arrived in Mexico.[6]

Because Borlaug had been a catalyst for change and helped to keep millions of people in Mexico from starving, the governments of India and Pakistan asked him to help them. India's population growth was outpacing its ability to grow enough crops to feed its citizens. Once they started using the seeds Borlaug had developed in Mexico, the crisis in India was also averted.

For his work in making a difference, Borlaug has been called the Father of the Green Revolution. His scientific work has been credited with saving hundreds of millions of lives by preventing food shortages. There's even a 50 percent chance you and I have consumed grain descended from one of the varieties he developed.[7]

In 1970 Borlaug was awarded the Nobel Peace Prize for his contributions to the world food supply. The Nobel Committee said, "More than any other single person of this age, he has helped provide bread for a hungry world."[8] Committee chair Aase Lionæs quoted Borlaug: "I am impatient and do not accept the need for slow change and evolution to improve the agriculture and food production of the emerging countries. . . . There is no time to be lost, considering the magnitude of the world food and population problem."[9] The keys to that change were the small, quiet actions Borlaug took day after day. It's telling that when notification of his winning the prize arrived at Borlaug's home at four o'clock in the morning, it missed him. He had already left earlier that morning to work in the wheat field, continuing to perform tests on the crops.

CHANGE DOESN'T HAPPEN ON ITS OWN

Norman Borlaug was a person of action. He not only hurt enough to seek change, saw enough to desire change, learned enough that he wanted to change, and received enough to be able to change, but he also was active enough to *create* change. He became a catalyst, and the work he did not only changed *his* world but changed *our* world. And don't let his advanced degrees, his Nobel Peace Prize, or the size of his impact fool you. The work he did was often unseen and unsung. The small actions he took every day that made him a catalyst occurred in the fields under the hot sun, not in some ivory tower, yet they still changed his world.

> MANY THINGS IN LIFE JUST HAPPEN, BUT POSITIVE CHANGE ISN'T ONE OF THEM. CHANGING ANYTHING IN OUR WORLD REQUIRES SOMEONE TO BE THE CATALYST.

Underground Railroad conductor Harriet Tubman said, "Every great dream begins with a dreamer. Always remember, you have within you the strength, the patience, and the passion to reach for the stars to change the world." While that is true, to make the dream come true, you must also act. Many things in life *just happen*, but positive change isn't one of them. Changing anything in our world requires someone to be the catalyst.

When it comes to changing our world, the first person transformed is the catalyst—the agent of change—and then it expands. That doesn't happen unless it starts within an individual. Here's how becoming a catalyst developed in me.

CHANGE BEGINS WITH CARING: I WANT TO MAKE A DIFFERENCE

When you tell someone he or she can be a catalyst for change, it can sound intimidating. It might appear to be out of reach or too grandiose. C. W. Vanderbergh wrote,

To love the whole world
For me is no chore;
My only real problem's
My neighbor next door.[10]

But the truth is that caring often begins that simply. The beginnings of transformation are humble and within reach of anyone. It's simply thinking *I want to make a difference*. If you care, you have the potential to change your world.

Do you want to make a difference somewhere, somehow in your world? If your answer is yes, then you have what it takes to become a catalyst. When President John F. Kennedy launched the Peace Corps, he said that everyone has a change-the-world speech inside them. I believe you have a change-the-world seed inside of you. You just need to nurture it to grow.

> "EVERYONE HAS A CHANGE-THE-WORLD SPEECH INSIDE THEM."
> —PRESIDENT JOHN F. KENNEDY

CHANGE STANDS UP FOR A CAUSE: DOING SOMETHING THAT MAKES A DIFFERENCE

As the seed for change grows within you, it becomes more defined. You begin to understand what it is you need to do. You connect with a cause that is from the heart. And you begin to take action. You begin *doing* things that make a difference. Most of the time, those things are small, and that's okay. Embrace the wisdom that says, "Do not despise these small beginnings."[11] Small actions, made consistently, lead to big changes.

A friend took a small action that made a big difference in

another person's life in April 2020 during the COVID-19 pandemic. Kevin Rathel was in a hospital on life support in Orlando, Florida. Doctors had tried nearly everything they could to save him, but he was unresponsive, and it looked like he was going to die. But then my friend James Crocker saw a message on Facebook. Rathel's doctors wanted to try one last thing to save him: giving him plasma from someone who had recovered from COVID-19. They were looking for a donor. James decided that if he were the right blood type, he would take action. He was and he did. James drove to Orlando from his home in South Florida. And it worked. Within hours, Rathel was conscious and improving. By standing up and taking action, James had saved his life.

> SMALL ACTIONS, MADE CONSISTENTLY, LEAD TO BIG CHANGES.

Change Spreads from Me to We: With People Who Want to Make a Difference

As you work to make a difference and see change begin to occur, you will begin to change. How does this happen? Positive change leads us to a new beginning. Our hopes begin to be realized. Our efforts begin to be rewarded. Our hearts begin to be fulfilled. And our work will begin to be recognized by others.

At this point you can become a transformation magnet. You can attract others. You can be positively contagious to others who want to make a difference, even if they didn't know how to do it. But now they have an example: you! Seeing you make a difference makes them want to join you. The result? Coming together for a common cause becomes a force multiplier. Your efforts grow from *me* to *we*. This is when being a catalyst for change starts to become really exciting.

CHANGE STEPS FORWARD WITH URGENCY: AT A TIME WHEN IT MAKES A DIFFERENCE

The phrase "strike while the iron is hot" comes from the blacksmithing trade. Metalworkers understand that timing is crucial if they want to successfully manipulate metal. Steel, for instance, needs to be at the optimum temperature to be able to work it. If the metal is cold, it won't move at all when struck with a hammer. If it's not heated enough, even a lot of hammering will make only the smallest of changes. On the other hand, if the metal is too hot, it can melt, rendering it worthless. There is a very short window of a few seconds when the steel's temperature is just right. The smith must strike quickly, because the metal doesn't stay at the perfect temperature for very long.

Similarly, change won't occur unless you step forward and start taking action. If you lose the sense of urgency, your cause can become like cold steel. It won't move, and change will grind to a halt. So you need to seize whatever opportunities you have now, where you are, and make the most of them. Initiative on fire accomplishes more than knowledge on ice.

HOW YOU CAN BECOME A CATALYST FOR CHANGE

When I first decided I wanted to make a difference, I had no idea how to do it. I wasn't sure what I would do or where it would take me or how I would get there. I just knew I wanted to help people, so I started doing what I could. Mother Teresa said, "I alone cannot change the world, but I can cast a stone across the waters to create many ripples." Little did I know that those humble beginnings of just starting to do what I could were creating ripples. You can create ripples too. Here's how to get started:

CHANGE FROM GOOD INTENTIONS TO GOOD ACTIONS

As I write this, my dad, Melvin, is ninety-eight years old. He's always been my hero. I've learned a lot from Dad. When I was young, one of his favorite riddles to ask us kids was about five frogs sitting on a log. "Four decided to jump off. How many are left on the log?" he would ask.

The first time I answered, "One."

"No," Dad replied. "There are five. Deciding is not doing. You have to do more than decide. You have to take action!"

Thanks to those frogs on a log, I learned there's a huge difference between good intentions and good actions:

- People with *good intentions* want to add value to others but find reasons not to do it.
- People with *good actions* want to add value to others and find ways to do it.
- People with *good intentions* can be passive, inconsistent, and disappointing.
- People with *good actions* are deliberate, consistent, and willful.
- *Good actions* represent the dividing line between words and results.

We often hear about the haves and the have-nots. When it comes to making a difference and changing our world, we should probably be talking about the dos and the do-nots. We tend to want others to judge us on our intentions. But what ultimately matters isn't what we intend to do. It's what we actually do. How do we miss this? We rarely tell ourselves, "I'm never going to do this good thing." Instead, we tell ourselves, "I'm going to do this tomorrow." But when tomorrow comes, we don't follow through. Maybe we mean to, but we don't. That's why the biggest gap between failure and success is the distance between *I should* and *I did*.

> GOOD ACTIONS REPRESENT THE DIVIDING LINE BETWEEN WORDS AND RESULTS.

Management expert Peter Drucker said, "You cannot predict the future, but you can create it."[12] As a catalyst for change, that's what you do. You create a better future by following through. Don't settle for good intentions. They won't change the world. Focus on good actions.

> "YOU CANNOT PREDICT THE FUTURE,
> BUT YOU CAN CREATE IT."
> —PETER DRUCKER

BECOME A POSSIBILIST

Recently Rob shared with me a great book by professor and physician Hans Rosling that has shaped the way he thinks about creating change. I learned a new word along with a fantastic concept:

People often call me an optimist, because I show them the enormous progress they didn't know about. That makes me angry. I'm not an optimist. That makes me sound naive. I'm a very serious "possibilist." That's something I made up. It means someone who neither hopes without reason, nor fears without reason, someone who constantly resists the overdramatic worldview. As a possibilist, I see all this progress, and it fills me with conviction and hope that further progress is possible. This is not optimistic. It is having a clear and reasonable idea about how things are. It is having a worldview that is constructive and useful.

When people wrongly believe that nothing is improving, they may conclude that nothing we have tried so far is working and lose confidence in measures that actually work. I meet many such people, who tell me they have lost all hope for humanity. Or, they may become radicals, supporting drastic measures that are counter-productive when, in fact, the methods we already use to improve our world are working just fine. . . .

A solution that works for me is to persuade myself to keep two thoughts in my head at the same time.

It seems that when we hear someone say things are getting better, we think they are also saying "don't worry, relax" or even "look away." But when I say things are getting better, I am not saying those things at all. I am certainly not advocating looking away from the terrible problems in the world. I am saying that things can be both bad and better.[13]

What a great word: *possibilist*! Rosling's perspective is right. We need to both do something to change the world *and* see positive things happening in the world. When you think like a possibilist, you are actively on the lookout for the possibilities in the world. Sadly, most people could use *possibility therapy*. They're like the

MOST PEOPLE COULD USE *POSSIBILITY THERAPY.*

people Rosling described who either see nothing but doom and gloom in the world and lose hope, or they are blind or indifferent to the problems around them.

Are you a possibilist? If your answer to any of these questions is yes, then you are.

- Do I think progress is possible but not easy?
- Do I see things as they are but not get discouraged?
- Am I unwilling to look away from problems that move me?
- Am I willing to do what I can to make my world a better place?

My friend Marcus Buckingham says that leaders are rarely pessimists. To lead change, to be a catalyst, you have to believe you can make a difference. And that's good news, because you can. Just because it hasn't been done before doesn't mean you can't be the one to do it. Why shouldn't you be?

Many of the catalysts of the world are unknown, unsung heroes who are possibilists. Rob met one named Tiffany, a twelve-year-old girl, when he was visiting an extremely impoverished school in Lima, Peru. While waiting to go into a classroom, he was looking at student artwork hanging on the wall, and one picture really jumped out at him because it was so full of life and hope.

The artist was Tiffany, who was full of confidence and optimism. When she invited Rob and his team, which included a camera crew, to visit her home, he readily accepted. Wanting to better understand her community, they followed her into a squatter's district called San Juan de Lurigancho.

"The farther we walked, the poorer it got," Rob said. "As we arrived at her living space, a shack, the roof was literally being repossessed by a group of workers for lack of payment. Her father—an out-of-work artist—was passed out drunk. Her mother was gone, working one of her two jobs to try to keep the family fed. I saw the life and optimism drain out of Tiffany's face, replaced with shame and embarrassment. I was so broken for her."

Rob immediately asked the film crew to turn off the cameras. They paid for the roof to keep them from losing it, and he did his best to encourage her. In situations like these, Rob's heart makes him want to adopt a child like Tiffany, but he knows the best thing he can do is connect her with people and programs that give her opportunities to develop as a person.

So that's what he did. With that little bit of help and encouragement, Tiffany became the first person in her family to graduate from high school and go to college. It changed her world, and she could have gone anywhere and done anything. But Tiffany chose to stay in her hometown and be a catalyst for change. She started a school for children from struggling families called Estrellitas de Amor (Little Stars of Love). She is creating positive change in her community by allowing boys and girls that grew up in the slum where she was born to learn and grow so that they, too, can change their world. And her example so impacted her family that her father no longer drinks alcohol, and he supports his daughter by bringing lunch to the schoolchildren every day.

TAKE OWNERSHIP

In my book *Put Your Dream to the Test*, one of the first questions I recommend people ask themselves is this: Is my dream really *my* dream? Why? Because if the dream you intend to pursue isn't really yours, you won't own it. And if you don't own it, you won't do what it takes to achieve it. Your dream becomes your dream when you recognize the contribution you can make. The same is true for becoming a catalyst for change. Only if you own it will you be able to fulfill it.

I was reminded of this in 2011 when I met with the board of my nonprofit organization EQUIP. We had just celebrated the fantastic milestone of training five million leaders from every country in the world. When you finally achieve a major goal that you've been pursuing for well over a decade, the question is, what's next? The board and I were discussing what we should do next. Should we target training another million leaders to get to the six million mark? Should we celebrate our victory, shut down the organization, and call it a day?

That's what many of the board members wanted to do. But I had a strong sense that we were not done as an organization. Something had been stirring in me for several years, namely, to shift from training leaders to transforming leaders. The board members wanted to know more, but at the time I couldn't articulate it. I didn't know how we would do it. I didn't even know how to define transformation at that time, but I believed we should take action despite not having all the answers.

Some of my board members were with me 100 percent. If I sensed it, they were willing to support it. Most were willing to support me while giving some time to figure it out. But not everyone was. A couple of board members simply didn't see it and stepped off the board. That didn't lessen my love for them. But I had made a decision. Even if I had to go it alone, I would commit to transformation.

That's the day I became the owner of the vision. When I made the commitment, it was a tangible step toward becoming a catalyst. I've learned that whenever I feel a sense of conviction about an issue, I just need to start moving in the direction I believe I should go, even when I'm uncertain.

Someone who is a fantastic example of a change catalyst who takes ownership of his vision for change is actor, writer, director, and producer Tyler Perry. A couple of years ago he agreed to speak at a Live2Lead event hosted by the John Maxwell Company. Most people who have followed his career know that he grew up poor and abused in New Orleans. He began writing as a kind of therapy after watching an episode of *The Oprah Winfrey Show* in which she talked about the benefits of writing. Perry started his career by writing and performing in a play titled *I Know I've Been Changed*. The first time he staged it, no one came to watch it. But when he got a second chance, he became highly successful. Then Hollywood, and the rest of the nation, recognized him when he created the character Madea and played her in movies.

Perry is also the founder and owner of Tyler Perry Studios in Atlanta, Georgia, and has been recognized as the first African American to own a major film studio.[14] He once said, "I've never been one to knock on the door and say, 'Please let me in.' I have always tried to make my own way. I do not think change comes from asking people to let you in. I think change comes by becoming owners of studios, owners of projects, owners of content."[15]

Before Perry went on stage for his talk, we had a chance to talk about leadership, and he told me part of his story. In 2006 he bought property and built his first studio in Atlanta after the success of the early Madea films. He quickly outgrew the space, so he sold that property, purchased a larger location, and built a second studio. He outgrew that one too. So he bought a bigger site, where he could build a studio he thought he could never outgrow. Much to his surprise, that one was soon beyond capacity.

Perry told me that after he outgrew that studio, he thought, *I don't want to do this anymore.* The last thing he wanted to do was to have to build again. He just wanted to keep making movies and television shows. But then he thought about all the people who already worked for him and all the additional people he could employ. So he went looking for an even bigger space. In 2015 he bought part of Fort McPherson, a historic site in Atlanta. He spent four years building it out, making it one of the largest production facilities in the country, with twelve sound stages, two hundred acres of green space, a backlot, and offices.[16]

"When you can *afford* to quit, you *can't* afford to quit," Perry told me, explaining that when you've made it, you no longer *need* to do more. But that's when you *can* do more—more than you've ever done before. That's when you can make the greatest difference. His ownership of the vision to change the world has made it possible for him to impact thousands of lives. And his continued commitment means he will not only impact greater numbers in the future, he will leave a legacy that lives beyond him. His sense of purpose, his *why*, is bigger than he is, and it will outlive him.

> "LET US REMEMBER: ONE BOOK, ONE PEN, ONE CHILD, AND ONE TEACHER CAN CHANGE THE WORLD."
> —MALALA YOUSAFZAI

He is a living testament to a statement made by education activist Malala Yousafzai: "Let us remember: One book, one pen, one child, and one teacher can change the world."[17] Tyler Perry started as a kid with a pen and a dream. Look at him now.

USE YOUR PAST CHANGES AS INSPIRATION FOR FUTURE CHANGE

Whatever changes you have fought for and won in the past should inspire you to believe you can change again in the future. And those changes—even incremental internal changes—will help you to make changes in your world. The Greek philosopher Plutarch said, "What we achieve inwardly will change outer reality."

I'm a great believer in the idea of "I did it, so you can too." Why? Because I've seen myself change from people pleaser to leader. I've gone from being someone with destination disease to a lifelong learner who never expects to arrive—growth-oriented instead of goal-oriented. I've grown from being fundamentally selfish to someone who wants to add value to others. I've changed and that qualifies me to help others change. It also inspires a passion within me to help others change. We need to be changed to bring change to others. Dreams aren't measured by the size of the project but by the level of faith and the degree of change within the person leading it.

INVITE OTHERS TO JOIN THE CAUSE

When you become a catalyst for change, one of the most significant things you can do is invite others to join you in the cause. As soon as another person works with you and is influenced by what you're doing, you are a leader—a leader whose *why* is bigger than you. Martin Luther King Jr. said about the importance of leaders, when it comes to change: "May I stress the need for courageous, intelligent, and dedicated leadership. . . . Leaders of sound integrity. Leaders not in love with publicity, but in love with justice. Leaders not in love with money, but in love with humanity. Leaders who can subject their particular egos to the greatness of the cause."[18]

Please don't be intimidated or discouraged by King's description of the leaders needed for an important cause. You don't have to be someone of his caliber to make a difference. Leadership is influence—nothing more, nothing less. You can and should influence others to work alongside you. Change requires a diversity of talents and skills in order to be accomplished. Your job is to give everyone who joins you permission to operate in their gifting and invite them to be in the story. If you aren't a good public speaker, find someone who is. If you tend to be a skeptic, balance yourself by inviting someone who's optimistic. Why? None of us is as smart as all of us.

> WHEN YOU BECOME A CATALYST FOR CHANGE, ONE OF THE MOST SIGNIFICANT THINGS YOU CAN DO IS INVITE OTHERS TO JOIN YOU IN THE CAUSE.

We recommend you start by gathering friends and family. You already have influence with them, and you're certainly already like-minded, at least in some areas. If you're not sure how much influence you have, answer these questions by writing down the names of as many people as you can think of for each:

- Who listens when you talk?
- Who asks for your advice?
- Who respects your experience?
- Who follows your recommendations?
- Who seeks your opinion?

- Who enjoys working beside you?
- Who advocates for you?
- Who values your time?
- Who shares positive things about you with others?
- Who do you add value to?

These are the first people you should talk to about your cause. They are the most likely to join you because, as the Friendship Principle says in *Winning with People*, "All things being equal, people will work with people they like; all things not being equal, they still will." Here's how you can go about gathering them.

Share Your Passion

The most important thing you can do is speak from your heart about the change you want to make and what you want to do to try to create it. Let people know how important it is to you and why. Passion is contagious with like-minded people. Use it to paint the vision.

Ask What They Think

Once you've shared your passion, don't try to sell them on your cause. Instead, ask them what they think and really listen. Pay attention not only to their words but also to their body language. Ask follow-up questions. Try to gauge whether they connect with your idea, are unmoved by it, or are somewhere in between.

Invite Them to Improve Your Ideas

You know you don't have all the answers and so will they. Invite them to give you their ideas. They may be able to improve your ideas or offer even better ones. Asking for input also increases buy-in. If people are on the fence, the process of contributing ideas just might draw them in and increase their connection to you and the cause. When people contribute ideas, your dream becomes their dream.

Ask Whether It's Something You Can Do Together

As you finish a conversation about your cause, don't leave things ambiguous. Be bold. Ask if they would be willing to join you in making a difference. The people who change their world influence others to think, speak, and act in such a way that makes a positive difference in their lives and the lives of others. Don't leave that to chance. But if you have to convince them to see the vision, you will have to convince them to take action. You want a partner, not a prisoner. So gladly welcome the willing onto your team and allow the uncommitted to go their own way.

FOCUS ON WHAT YOU CAN DO

Billionaire philanthropist Bill Austin said, "We can't change everything, but we can change something."[19] The questions to ask are: What can *I* change? What can *I* do exceptionally well? What's *my* A-game? What do *I* do that consistently makes a positive impact? That's what you should be focusing on.

As you read those questions, what came to mind? Do you know with certainty where your focus should be? If not, maybe you need some perspective. Organizational psychologist Benjamin Hardy said, "True learning occurs when you can see the same thing with new eyes. They call this a Copernican Revolution. For example, when we as a people realized the sun did not revolve around the earth, but vice-versa. That single insight shifted how we saw everything. We were looking at the same stimulus but with a new frame."[20]

How can you develop a new frame? You need to try to look at yourself objectively. Your best contribution will be based on

- Your gifts
- Your past successes
- Your passions
- Your opportunities

Take some time to write down what these are. If you have difficulty identifying them, ask others who know you well to share their observations. Then try to figure out how they add up.

Why is this important? There are several reasons. First, what you focus on expands.

> YOU WILL NEVER BE WHAT YOU OUGHT TO BE UNTIL YOU ARE DOING WHAT YOU OUGHT TO BE DOING.

Second, what you focus on shapes how you view yourself; it impacts your future. Third, you will never be what you ought to be until you are doing what you ought to be doing.

DO SOMETHING

Rob's dad, Bob, founded OneHope in 1987, and he has always understood the importance of taking action. Rob has often heard his dad say, "Just do *something*!" When someone would present a pressing need to Bob, his response was always, "So what are *you* going to do about it?" His dad's example of seeing a need *and* taking action has influenced how Rob leads OneHope and the many other initiatives and movements he is a part of. In the words of Duane Mellor, a leader who helped implement the positive changes in Avondale, "The smallest deed is greater than the largest intention."

Now is the time to *do* something. It's okay to start even when you don't have all the answers. Do what you know to do. You don't need to know every step of the way. There is no silver bullet. There is no perfect plan. Focus on purpose, not perfection. There is no standing still when it comes to making a difference. You are either moving forward or sliding backward. Start moving forward. And invite others to join you. If you don't, you may look back a year from now and wish you had started today. When I started EQUIP, I had no idea we would train millions of leaders. When Rob took over OneHope, he didn't know the organization would be able to help children in nearly every country in the world. We just took steps forward, hoping to make a difference.

> "THE SMALLEST DEED IS GREATER THAN THE LARGEST INTENTION."
> —DUANE MELLOR

Your goal is to make things better however you can. Think about what *better* can do. Incremental change is better than the status quo. Author and ServiceMaster chairman emeritus William Pollard said, "Without change there is no innovation, creativity, or incentive for improvement. Those who initiate change will have a better opportunity to manage the change that is inevitable." Would you rather have a hand in positive change or just be swept along in the negative change that is going to happen without you? We would rather be catalysts for positive change without preconditions. We believe you would too.

A HEART FOR BANGLADESH

When you are willing to take small steps and become a catalyst, there's really no telling what it can lead to or how great an impact you might make. If you had asked Maria Conceicao when she was a girl what kind of impact she would make on others, I doubt she could have dreamed of doing a fraction of what she's actually done.

I met Maria in Dubai at a conference where both of us were slated to speak. She told me some of her story, and it blew me away. We started to develop a friendship, and when I got home, I did some research to find out more about her.

Maria was born in Avanca, a small village in Portugal. When she was two years old, her mother, who was ill, went to Lisbon to find work, and Maria was left to stay with an Angolan immigrant named Maria Cristina Matos who worked as a cleaning woman.[21] Sadly, Maria's mother never returned from Lisbon. Despite having six children of her own to feed and care for, Matos raised Maria as her own, even going against authorities who wanted to take the child away and put her in foster care.[22]

When Maria was nine, Matos died. By the time Maria was twelve she had to quit school and go to work, cleaning houses, to support herself. She threw herself into her work. "I thought, if I have to be a cleaner, then I will be the best cleaner around," said Maria. She worked hard, but she also had dreams of traveling the world. At eighteen, she left her home country in search of a better life. She worked hard, learned English and French, and started getting better employment in restaurants. Eventually, while in England, she applied for a position as a flight attendant with Emirates airlines, based out of Dubai, and she got the job.[23]

Her work took her to, among other places, Bangladesh. What she saw there struck her, both bringing her pain and inspiring her. "In 2005, I was in Dhaka and I visited the slums," she said. "They were living in makeshift homes that were surrounded by so much garbage and filth. The scarcity of resources and livelihood in slums were drastic, so I started to help, just in a small way to start."

Maria was especially struck by the plight of girls there. Typically, they were treated like property and married off by their families by age thirteen. By eighteen, they usually had four or five children and were trapped in poverty for life.

Rather than walking away, Maria decided to do something. "[I began by] taking all of my holidays in Bangladesh. I promised 101 families with 600 students between them that I would do everything I could to take their children out of poverty, slavery, and destitution. Many people in Dubai helped me [with] building up the community and several facilities, including a school."[24]

Maria worked with corporate sponsors and influential people in Dubai to help the poor in Bangladesh. But when the 2009 recession hit, donations and funding disappeared overnight. She didn't let that stop her. Now that she had become a catalyst for change, she was not going to let anything stop her from making a difference. Looking for another way to raise money, she turned to the internet. She discovered that her best way forward would be to do something to get noticed and use charity campaigns to raise funds. With no experience and no special athletic talent, she trained to climb a mountain, and in 2010 she summited Mount Kilimanjaro.

But that didn't get the attention she had hoped for, so she set her sights on another target. In 2011 she trekked to the North

Pole. She was the first Portuguese woman in the world to do it. That year she also walked a marathon in each of the seven emirates of the United Arab Emirates in seven days.[25]

She was able to gain enough attention that a prominent school in Dubai provided scholarships for five children from the slums of Dhaka for an education up to the age of eighteen.[26] But she was also frustrated that the impact of her efforts was so short-lived.[27] She decided she needed to do something really big. She would climb Mount Everest. After training for a year, she made the attempt and reached the summit in 2013. "It was not for glory that I had set out on this expedition," said Maria. "It was a desperate measure . . . to help slum children in Dhaka. I wanted to let them live with dignity and give them the opportunities I had when I was young."[28] Though she missed her goal of raising a million dollars from her climb, she did start gaining attention for her cause.

With that success behind her, she ramped up her efforts, taking on one amazing feat after another. Her main gift was not athletic talent but sheer determination. She holds multiple Guinness World Records, including most consecutive days running an official ultramarathon by a female and fastest time to run an ultramarathon on each continent by a female.[29] After that, she started doing Ironman competitions. She even attempted to swim the English Channel—only a year after learning to swim. She described herself as "this little village girl from a poor background doing this crazy challenge."[30] But her efforts have paid off. After fifteen years, the older students she helped are now in universities around the world.

Inspired by Maria's story, I invited her to speak to three thousand of my coaches in Orlando. She was so passionate that everybody in the room was inspired to support her cause. In a matter of minutes they donated $150,000. But her road hasn't been easy. She said it has always been a challenge "to be taken seriously in countries or societies where women are not supposed to be strong or taken seriously as leaders." And specifically, in Bangladesh, she said you really have to "prove yourself, prove that you are right. You have to be a woman of action, and I think it's the same in the rest of the world. Action is what gets things done."[31] Spoken like a true catalyst.

> I EXPERIENCE SOMETHING SO LIFE-CHANGING THAT I CHANGE. I SHARE SOMETHING SO LIFE-CHANGING THAT YOU CHANGE. WE FACILITATE SOMETHING SO LIFE-CHANGING THAT OTHERS CHANGE.

Maria Conceicao has experienced the change cycle and become a catalyst. So did Norman Borlaug and Tyler Perry and Tiffany from Peru. Each of them has a different skill set, a different background, but they are all making a difference. And so can you. The change cycle goes like this:

I experience something so life-changing that I change.

I share something so life-changing that you change.

We facilitate something so life-changing that others change.

The process begins with you. The scale of what you do doesn't matter. If you're willing to embrace change yourself and take action, the transformation process has already begun. You've already started to become a catalyst. And you can change your world.

CHAPTER 3

WE ALL NEED
ONE ANOTHER

*I can do what you cannot, and you can do what
I cannot; together we can do great things.*
—MOTHER TERESA[1]

On March 25, 2020, Sam Yoder, a company owner in Berlin, Ohio, received a phone call from a business friend in Akron. This was during the rise of the COVID-19 pandemic. The previous December, officials in China had confirmed that a mystery illness with pneumonia-like symptoms was affecting dozens of people in the city of Wuhan. Less than two weeks after that, the Chinese state media reported the first known death from what was being called a coronavirus. That virus spread quickly to other countries around the world in January, even as Chinese authorities shut down Wuhan later in the month. Cases broke out in Europe, other parts of Asia, the Middle East, the United States, and eventually South America. It was declared a pandemic by the World Health Organization on March 12.[2]

STAY AT HOME IN ISOLATION?

On March 22, Mike DeWine, the governor of Ohio, where Sam lived, gave a stay-at-home order for the state. Included in that order was a directive to close all nonessential businesses. That included Sam's company, Berlin Gardens, a manufacturer of patio furniture, gazebos, firepits, and other outdoor items. That was a painful directive for Sam. It meant he had to close the doors to his business and send everyone home. Despite the fact that he would have to go without revenue, he was trying to figure out how to pay all of his employees for forty hours a week while he was closed. "One of the beliefs I have is to take care of our people first, and everything else will fall into place," said Sam.[3]

When TKM Print Solutions, a print, sign, and custom fabrication shop, contacted Sam, he got excited. With the coronavirus raging across the country, there was a shortage of plastic face shields for medical workers. The need was for *millions* of them. TKM wanted to do something to solve that problem, but it couldn't do it alone. It could provide the materials needed to manufacture shields, but they didn't have the manpower or the facilities to produce them. Sam's employees at Berlin Gardens were used to working with plastic. They normally manufactured furniture from recycled plastic. The question being asked was whether they would be willing to work together with TKM to produce the face shields? Sam thought this might be a way to keep his employees working.

That afternoon, Sam, his management team, and staff from TKM immediately drove to the parking lot of a nearby home improvement store to discuss it. They found out the need for face shields was greatest in Connecticut, with a request for 150,000 masks by March 30, which was in only five days![4] They discussed whether it might be possible, and Sam's hope rose. Though it seemed daunting, this might be a way not only to keep his staff employed but also to make a difference during the pandemic.

OR WORK TOGETHER?

The next morning, Sam and his team met at the Berlin Gardens facility to try to figure out how they could pull it off. Could they convert the space from manufacturing furniture to making face shields? They set up a production line of tables and made forty masks to test the process. It looked like it might work, so they sent those masks to Connecticut to be inspected to make sure they were up to the needed standard.

When Sam received the approval, he got the word out to his employees, and they came in to work. Meanwhile, TKM started shipping in the four-feet-by-eight-feet clear plastic sheets needed to create shields. They went into production with all their nearly one hundred employees. They didn't quite hit that first 150,000 goal, but they *were* able to produce nearly 90,000 face shields by March 30. Some of those masks went to Yale New Haven Hospital.[5]

With all of Sam's employees back to work, they were soon producing between thirty and thirty-five thousand shields a day, boxing them, and preparing them for shipment—all while maintaining social distancing rules. The money the company was receiving for manufacturing the shields almost covered Sam's payroll, which he would have been paying his people for staying home. So it was a real win-win. But that wasn't the best part of it.

Sam's employees, who were used to working scattered across

seven buildings, were all working together in a single facility. People saw one another every day who normally didn't, and they were able to rekindle friendships. They talked together while they worked. Sam would move around talking to everyone, finding out how they were doing, asking if there were ways to improve the manufacturing process, getting advice from them on how to work better, smarter, faster. Everyone felt involved and shared a strong sense of community.

To inspire them, Sam put up big screens with their goals for the day that updated every time they finished another box of shields. It made them want to work harder, and Sam told them if they hit the goal early, they could go home but would be paid through the end of the day. Sam told them, "We are on the front lines of a war. Every shield you make protects the first responders and others against the bullets of the virus." At their peak, they were producing a shield every fifteen seconds. Everyone had the sense that they were making a real difference. They were saving lives.

Sam said the whole effort gave his community the lift it needed; it made them feel like they were defeating the virus. The feelings were so strong that other people from the community came in every evening, bringing food for the workers who made the shields all day. Not only that, but many of these members of the community asked if they could volunteer to get on the assembly line and make face shields too! They often stayed and worked until eight o'clock in the evening, just to be a part of the experience of changing their world.

"We feel humbled and

> "THE ONLY THING THAT LIMITS US IN A TIME OF CRISIS IS OUR LACK OF CREATIVITY. THAT AND RECOGNIZING THAT WE ALL NEED ONE ANOTHER."
> —SAM YODER

blessed that we can be a part of this endeavor to help provide protection for those who are on the front lines!" said Sam. "To go from not knowing how long we can cover our payroll to having enough income to cover payroll plus helping the medical industry is truly amazing."

Sam is a good man and a good leader. The work he, his employees, TKM, and all the others accomplished is a testament to what can be done when people are willing to work together. Sam said, "The only thing that limits us in a time of crisis is our lack of creativity." Along with creativity, we need to recognize that we all need one another.

Transformational Truths

As we work to become catalysts of change on any scale, we don't want to miss what happens when we work with others to accomplish the vision. Everything multiplies. The greater the vision and the more difficult the cause, the more we need people to work together to accomplish it. The Law of Significance in *The 17 Indisputable Laws of Teamwork* says, "One is too small a number to achieve greatness." You can make changes in your world on your own—no doubt about it. But if the work you're doing to make a difference starts to grow, you will need others to work alongside you to keep it going and make it better. And if you're leading that group of people, you have to realize the team and the transformation they are creating are essential to realizing success. Everyone working together is valuable, and we all need one another.

As you link up with others to make a difference, keep the following thoughts in mind.

WE IS MORE IMPORTANT THAN ME

When I received my first leadership position at age twenty-two, my first thought was, *I want to make a difference.* I can still remember the joy I felt as I did my very best to help and add value to people. My energy increased, my vision expanded, and my desire to help grew bigger each day. I was loving what I was doing. Over time, my passion to make a difference collided with the reality that I was limited in how many people I could add value to if I tried to do everything myself.

Entrepreneur and LinkedIn cofounder Reid Hoffman said, "No matter how brilliant your mind or strategy, if you're playing a solo game, you'll always lose out to a team."[6] So the first question you need to ask yourself is, "Am I ready to play on the transformation team?"

> "NO MATTER HOW BRILLIANT YOUR MIND OR STRATEGY, IF YOU'RE PLAYING A SOLO GAME, YOU'LL ALWAYS LOSE OUT TO A TEAM."
> —REID HOFFMAN

The odds of success in any endeavor increase dramatically when you team up with other people. Leadership consultant and speaker Gustavo Razzetti noted, "A study by the Association for Training and Development (ATD) found that you are 65 percent more likely to meet a goal after committing to another person. If you also establish an ongoing partnership, your chances increase to 95 percent."[7]

A group of people becomes a team that can make a difference when the majority of its members make the transition from thinking "The group is here to benefit me" to "I'm here to benefit the group." Management consultant Richard Barrett said, "The fundamental change that occurs during cultural transformation is a shift in attitude from 'What's in it for us (me)?' to 'What's best for the common good?' There is a shift in focus from 'I' to 'We.'"[8] When this happens, we are more likely to accept letting ourselves down instead of letting the team down.

The necessary shift from working alone to working with others isn't just something that's needed in business or the non-profit world. You can even see it at work in nature. Wolves gather in packs and lions in prides to live, hunt, and defend themselves. Geese flying in formation increase their range by approximately 70 percent.[9] And domesticated animals, such as horses, team up to accomplish more together. It's said that a champion-caliber horse can pull a sled weighing forty-five hundred pounds. If you hitch that horse together with another horse—even one not as capable—they can pull much more than double that amount: twelve thousand pounds. And four horses working together multiplies the productivity with the ability to pull over thirty thousand pounds!

I love something Chuck Swindoll wrote years ago that communicates the importance of a group of people working together:

> Nobody is a whole chain. Each one is a link. But take away one link and the chain is broken.
>
> Nobody is a whole team. Each one is a player. But take away one player and the game is forfeited.
>
> Nobody is a whole orchestra. Each one is a musician. But take away one musician and the symphony is incomplete. . . .
>
> You guessed it. We need each other. You need someone and someone needs you. Isolated islands we're not. To make this thing called life work, we gotta lean and support. And

relate and respond. And give and take. And confess and forgive. And reach out and embrace. And release and rely. . . .

Since none of us is a whole, independent, self-sufficient, supercapable, all-powerful hotshot, let's quit acting like we are. Life's lonely enough without our playing that silly role.

The game's over. Let's link up.[10]

There is truth in the old adage that team means Together—Everyone—Accomplishes—More. If you want to change the world and be part of a transformation movement, you need to put *we* ahead of *me*. You need to be willing to link up with others.

TEAM MEANS TOGETHER—EVERYONE— ACCOMPLISHES—MORE.

WHO IS MORE IMPORTANT THAN HOW

Once you've landed the idea that the cause and the team are more important than you as an individual, the next question you need to answer is "Who do I need to team up with?" This was a hard lesson for me to learn. I knew early in my life that I wanted to help people. I thought, *I want to make a difference.* As soon as I realized that making a difference would require the help of others, my thought expanded to *I want to make a difference with people.* And I started recruiting people to get on board to help me with my cause. The good news was that I was able to gather people to me because of my passion and personality. The bad news was that not everyone I got on board was there to be part of the cause. Some just wanted to go along for the ride.

Have you ever watched a rowing team work together? In the

largest boats, called sculls, eight athletes row in unison, with a coxswain in the stern of the boat steering and calling out the cadence of their strokes. These teams can only succeed if they work together. In my early days of leadership, I was gathering people to fill every seat of the boat, but only a couple of us were rowing. The rest were just sitting back, relaxing, and enjoying the ride.

Understanding this, I made another shift in my thinking to *I want to make a difference with people who want to make a difference.* I finally grasped that *who* was more important than *how* when it comes to working with people to change the world. If we wanted to make a difference, we had to be fighting for the same cause. That taught me to become more selective about who I teamed up with.

That decision didn't please everybody around me, which was challenging for me at first. As I mentioned previously, I was a people pleaser early in my career. When people criticized my choices, I fought the old people pleaser inside of me by thinking of what Theodore Roosevelt, the twenty-sixth president of the United States, said about critical people:

> It is not the critic who counts: not the man who points out how the strong man stumbles or where the doer of deeds could have done better. The credit belongs to the man who is actually in the arena, whose face is marred by dust and sweat and blood, who strives valiantly, who errs and comes up short again and again, because there is no effort without error or shortcoming, but who knows the great enthusiasms, the great devotions, who spends himself for a worthy cause; who, at the best, knows, in the end, the triumph of high achievement, and who, at the worst, if he fails, at least he fails while daring greatly, so that his place shall never be with those cold and timid souls who knew neither victory nor defeat.[11]

I like what author, speaker, and professor Brené Brown observed about Roosevelt's quote. She wrote:

> Going back to Roosevelt's "Man in the Arena" speech, I also learned that the people who love me, the people I really depend on, were never the critics who were pointing at me while I stumbled. They weren't in the bleachers at all. They were with me in the arena. Fighting for me and with me.
>
> Nothing has transformed my life more than realizing that it's a waste of time to evaluate my worthiness by weighing the reaction of the people in the stands. The people who love me and will be there regardless of the outcome are within arm's reach. This realization has changed everything.[12]

When you partner with the right people—people who are on the same page, who have the same values, who are willing to work for the same cause, who will fight for one another—it makes all the difference in the world

Who should you team up with to transform your world? We'd recommend that you start by looking for people who are already doing something about the cause that calls to you. Is there an existing organization that's already engaged in the cause that you could join or partner with? If so, you may not need to reinvent the wheel. If you share a common cause and there's also a values match, then join with them to make a difference. (In chapter 6, Rob and I will tell you about our experience of seeing lives changed at transformation tables. We'll give you an opportunity to jump in there at no cost. You may want to start there.)

On the other hand, you may be the one who needs to start gathering people together. Start by approaching people in your immediate network, and then expand beyond it. What connections do your connections have? Who do you know who knows someone you might want to know? Use what's called the small-world phenomenon, or six degrees of separation, to your advantage. Rob talked to me about this. The idea was developed by psychologist Stanley Milgram in the 1960s. It's the idea that one person can connect with any other person in the world through only six intermediaries.[13] Only now, Rob says that instead of 6 "degrees" between people, thanks largely to social media, there are really only 3.2 degrees of separation between any two people in the world.

What is the significance of the small-world phenomenon? Whether you're a catalytic leader trying to gather a like-minded group of people to become a team or you're an individual who wants to make a difference looking to join a group, team, or organization that's already doing something, you can find others to work with. Start by connecting with people you know well, then broaden your scope to those you barely know, and keep exploring connections until you find the right people.

That's what my nonprofit organizations did when we committed to starting a transformation movement in Guatemala. We found Guatemala Próspera, a well-led local nonprofit organization that wanted to see their country transformed, and we worked with their leaders. We came up with a strategy that could positively impact

> "NOTHING HAS TRANSFORMED MY LIFE MORE THAN REALIZING THAT IT'S A WASTE OF TIME TO EVALUATE MY WORTHINESS BY WEIGHING THE REACTION OF THE PEOPLE IN THE STANDS."
> —BRENÉ BROWN

people in the country and that we believed would start a transformation movement. We knew that if we could teach values to 10 percent of the people in the country, and they became committed to embracing and living those values, it could create a tipping point for the nation.[14] But we all agreed that the best way to reach 10 percent of the population was not to focus on how many people we trained but on *who* we trained. We worked to recruit the top leaders in the following eight streams of influence: government, education, business, religion, media, arts, sports, and health care. We believed that if we could influence them, they would influence others. It's still too early in the process to see if we can reach that tipping point, but so far the strategy is working, and we hope in time to see Guatemala transform.

> "IT'S NOT THE LOAD THAT WEIGHS YOU DOWN, IT'S THE WAY YOU CARRY IT."
> —UNKNOWN

As someone once remarked, "It's not the load that weighs you down, it's the way you carry it." When you invite other people to join you in carrying the burden of transformation, it lightens the load and makes the journey enjoyable.

WHAT UNITES US IS GREATER THAN WHAT DIVIDES US

One of the most important questions you need to ask as soon as you connect with other people is "Do we have a values match?" The Law of Identity in *The 17 Indisputable Laws of Teamwork* says "Shared values define the team." If your values and the values of the people on the team match, you will experience alignment, unity, and effectiveness. If not, you will never feel like there is a fit; you and they will remain frustrated.

Having common values among team members versus not having them is like the difference between a herd of horses and a herd of donkeys when they're under pressure. Horse trainer Stephen Brown said that when a group of horses encounter a threat, they stand in a circle facing each other with their hind legs pointing outward, ready to kick at their enemy. Donkeys, on the other hand, do just the opposite. They face the threat, but that means when they do kick, they strike each other.[15]

Once you've determined there is an alignment of values, focus on what you have in common, not your differences. What we focus on expands. If we focus on our differences, our differences increase. If we focus on what unites us, then our unity increases. President John F. Kennedy promoted unity when he said, "Let both sides explore what problems unite us instead of belaboring the problems which divide us."[16]

> "LET BOTH SIDES EXPLORE WHAT PROBLEMS UNITE US INSTEAD OF BELABORING THE PROBLEMS WHICH DIVIDE US."
> —JOHN F. KENNEDY

We saw a fantastic example of opposing sides coming together last year when I went to Paraguay with a large group of volunteer coaches from the John Maxwell Team to launch a phase of my values-based youth program in public schools called iLead. While there, I was invited to speak to one of the country's most popular soccer teams, Cerro Porteño. They embraced the good values we taught and began teaching them to their teams, their youth soccer programs, and even their fan clubs. They saw such remarkable results.

What happened next was even more remarkable. Cerro

Porteño decided to share the values training program with one of their rival teams, Club Olimpia, and they began using transformation tables to teach values throughout their system too. They were so excited about it that they shared the materials with another rival team, Club Libertad, who is currently introducing values transformation tables in their organization.

If you're a fan of soccer, you know that rivalries between teams can be fierce, but all soccer fans also share a brotherhood and sisterhood that binds them. These rival teams are looking past their competitive differences because they want to do something great for their community. If they work together to change their communities, they have a chance to change their nation.

At the signing of the Declaration of Independence, Benjamin Franklin reputedly said, "We all must hang together or we will hang separately." The Founding Fathers were a diverse group with different backgrounds and professions from different locations. Though they shared a common language, they identified as citizens of their states, not the common country they were trying to form. It was no accident that they called themselves the United States. But they focused on their common desire for liberty. That is what bound them together, and they knew that if they didn't remain united, they would lose their cause.

WHAT I HAVE IS MORE IMPORTANT THAN WHAT I LACK

The next question you need to ask yourself is, "What assets can I bring to a transformation team?" You may think those assets are obvious, or you may question whether you can contribute anything of real value. But the truth is, you have value and bring value to any team. Don't try to be someone you're not or wish for abilities you don't have. Leverage the strengths you already possess and build on them to benefit others. As poet Edwin Markham wrote,

> There is a destiny that makes us brothers:
> None goes his way alone:
> All that we send into the lives of others
> Comes back into our own.[17]

We can add value to our teammates as they add value to us, and together we can add enough value to our world to change it.

What are your contributions to the cause? What qualities can you bring to the table to make a difference? If you are having trouble figuring out your gifting, take a look at the following list of assets and rate yourself on a scale of one (weakest) to five (strongest) for each:

Passion
Experience
Knowledge
Skills
Relationships
Influence
Vision
Time
Resources

The Law of the Niche in *The 17 Indisputable Laws of Teamwork* says, "All players have a place where they add the most value." You have a unique role to take and unique contributions to make if you can find them. When you do, you make the team stronger, more complete.

We told you about Rob's experience in Avondale in chapter 1. Time after time he has seen people give to others from whatever they have. For example, he has seen elderly people from the senior center near Avondale go across the street to help small children every week by reading to them. These seniors give what they have to give.

> "SHE'S GOT GAPS, I GOT GAPS, TOGETHER WE FILL GAPS."
> —SYLVESTER STALLONE AS ROCKY BALBOA

To some it may seem like a small thing, but they are helping these children to learn to read better and are providing needed consistency to the lives of these children.

Everyone can do something, and when they do, it makes it better for everyone. I like the way Rocky Balboa in the Academy Award–winning movie *Rocky* expresses this idea. Talking about Adrian, his girlfriend, he said, "She's got gaps, I got gaps, together we fill gaps."[18]

COLLABORATION IS MORE IMPORTANT THAN COOPERATION

We currently live in a time of hostility, division, and partisanship. People would rather draw lines and throw stones than engage in conversation and try to find solutions together. In this climate, cooperation may seem like the best we can hope for between people. But that's selling ourselves short. We can do better.

Cooperation is unity for the sake of unity. Cooperation says, "Let's just get along or else nothing will get done." Collaboration is unity for the sake of shared vision. Collaboration says, "Let's work together because this *has* to be done."

We believe the implication of cooperation is that people are *not* working *against* one another. But when there is true collaboration, they *are* working *for* one another. They are intentionally going in the same direction, helping one another to achieve something they all feel is worthwhile.

We see this kind of collaboration between schools in Paraguay. I mentioned that we launched iLead there. As part of the program, students were encouraged to do projects related to the values they're learning. A school in the program initiated contact with another school in the community to plan how to beautify their town square. Together they picked up trash, painted buildings, and planted flowers. Before long, schools in surrounding communities saw what had happened and started their own projects to beautify their town squares. That has turned into a statewide challenge where schools are competing to do the most for their districts. They are doing more than cooperating. They're collaborating.

> COOPERATION SAYS, "LET'S JUST GET ALONG OR ELSE NOTHING WILL GET DONE." COLLABORATION SAYS, "LET'S WORK TOGETHER BECAUSE THIS HAS TO BE DONE."

When we all work together in collaboration, everyone benefits. I love the image of how coastal redwood trees grow as an example of collaboration. Unlike many other trees that put down relatively deep roots, including a taproot, coastal redwoods don't. Even though the trees can grow to be nearly four hundred feet tall, their roots are shallow, going down only six to twelve feet. But they spread out broadly—often to more than one hundred feet. And they grow in groves, with their roots interweaving together, making the trees stand strong together, even in violent storms. Though they are the tallest trees in the world, redwoods rarely fall. No wonder they've been known to live for longer than two thousand years![19]

Rob has studied a method of collaboration called collective impact. It was first introduced in 2011 by John Kania, the managing director at Foundation Strategy Group, and Mark Kramer, a professor at the John F. Kennedy School of Government at Harvard University. They developed it to try to solve large, complex, diverse social problems. It fosters a kind of collective collaboration that includes five important agreements, which we've adapted:

- A common agenda
- A shared measurement system
- Contributing activities
- Continuous communication
- A support team

Let's take a look at each of them.

A COMMON AGENDA

The starting point for collaboration is an agreement on what the problem is and on how everyone will work together to solve it. Without this common agenda, it's impossible for everyone to work together proactively and go in the same direction.

Moving together for a common cause will always bring about important changes. Often one of those changes becomes the keystone that makes even greater changes possible. In architecture, a keystone is the piece that makes an arch or vault possible. Author and businessman Greg Satell wrote, "Identifying that keystone change is the first major challenge of any change movement, and until you meet that challenge, your efforts will likely be in vain."[20] Satell cites examples of keystone events that facilitated movements. In 1930, Mahatma Gandhi organized a salt march—a disruptive but nonviolent demonstration—to protest the British monopoly on salt. With eighty other protesters, he started walking from his home in Sabarmati toward the sea.[21] They walked twenty-four days, and as they did, others joined them. By the time they reached Dandi on the Arabian Sea, thousands of additional protesters had joined them. Gandhi illegally harvested salt there. "With this," he announced, "I am shaking the foundations of the British Empire."[22] Gandhi's protest sparked the protests of millions of people all across India. In the end, the March to the Sea was the keystone event that ultimately led to India's independence from Britain. Without the common agenda of peaceful protest against the salt monopoly, this significant change might not have been possible.

A SHARED MEASUREMENT SYSTEM

How do you know you're actually accomplishing anything? You measure your progress, and you don't leave the *how* of the measuring up in the air. You *define* it, and everyone agrees on what constitutes success and how it will be specifically measured. You will read more about this in chapter 8.

CONTRIBUTING ACTIVITIES

Artist Vincent van Gogh said, "Great things are done by a series of small things brought together."[23] One of the great marks of collaboration is that everyone actively works together, not for the sake of activity, but by doing only what moves the ball forward and creates progress for the cause. Unity of mission doesn't mean uniformity of action.

Rob points out that the most important aspect of this concept is that everything that everyone does for the cause works together with everything everyone else does for it. This idea is sometimes called *reinforcing activities* by theorists or *irreducible complexity* by engineers. It's the idea that all the parts are functioning and working together simultaneously, each doing its own job.

CONTINUOUS COMMUNICATION

The Law of Communication in *The 17 Indisputable Laws of Teamwork* says "interaction fuels action." If a group of people want to be successful working together, they need to keep talking to one another. One of my mentors, Charles Blair, warned me about the danger of miscommunication when he said to me, "Have an understanding so there is not a misunderstanding." Often miscommunication is a result of differing assumptions. The word *communication* comes from the Latin word *communis,* which means common. Communication gets better when people have a common cause *and* they talk to one another continuously to make sure they keep it in common.

> "HAVE AN UNDERSTANDING SO THERE IS NOT A MISUNDERSTANDING."
> —CHARLES BLAIR

A SUPPORT TEAM

Everyone who is working to advance the cause becomes more effective when supported by a team of people dedicated to the task of coordinating efforts, assisting their needs, and facilitating communication. In academic circles, they call this a *backbone organization*. We prefer to think of it as a support team—staff or volunteers who work to help keep everything going and in the right direction. In a connected and networked world, the support of a team is indispensable.

If you are gathering people to a cause, then make sure you develop a skilled support team, communicate continuously with people, align them into contributing activities, agree on how you will specifically measure progress, and work toward a common agenda.

Winning Together

Someone who understands transformation and teamwork is my friend Casey Crawford. I had heard about him before I ever met him because of his positive reputation in the business world and the meteoric success of his company. The John Maxwell Team recognized Casey with the Transformation Leadership Award, and I got to know him over a three-hour lunch. He is doing amazing things.

Casey grew up in Maryland and Virginia near Washington, DC, at a time when the city was known as the murder capital of the country. He worked in his father's hardware stores in some of the most depressed neighborhoods in the area. "If you were a child born into poverty in the District during that time the outlook was bleak," he later observed.

Casey also played sports. He was a good-enough football player to get a scholarship to Virginia, where he played tight end. That was followed by a brief three-year NFL career. He managed to sign with the Carolina Panthers as an undrafted rookie. But in his third season, Casey was cut by the Panthers at the end of training camp and picked up by the Tampa Bay Buccaneers. At the end of Casey's first practice in Florida, Tampa Bay head coach Jon Gruden gathered the team into a tight circle and said, "We are going to win a world championship, we are going to do it with this group of men, and we are going to do it this year."

What Gruden said came true. "The season was a magical one and it culminated in a Super Bowl championship," said Casey. "After the game I found myself on a stage on the fifty-yard-line singing "It's My Life" with Bon Jovi, my arm around my wife, and my hand on the Lombardi Trophy. Although I had done very little to contribute to our success that season, I felt a completion of my goals for football."

On the plane ride home, Casey made a decision. At age twenty-five, he would retire from the NFL. As Casey expressed it, he wanted to "transition my life from entertainment to impact." He wanted to make a difference in the world.

A Heart for People and a Head for Business

With a heart to help people, Casey began to search for a way to add value to people. In addition to being good at sports, Casey also had a knack for business and had always been a bit of an entre-preneur: he remembers going door to door to sell papier-mâché fans in first grade to make money. During his NFL off-seasons in Charlotte, North Carolina, he used to get up at six in the morning to run and lift weights. By nine he was done and had the rest of the day open ahead of him. In that free time, he started to buy houses, fix them up, and rent them. He was doing pretty well—so well that someone wanted to borrow money from him in a short-term loan. He didn't want to take the risk, so he initially said no. But his wife, Michelle, a recent law school graduate, told him there would be a way to write the loan that would protect them, so they lent the money. Casey said he didn't sleep for the next thirty days—the period of the loan.

In the five years after retiring from football, Casey moved back to North Carolina and worked in real estate, banking, and the mortgage industry in Charlotte. By then he had a vision for how he wanted to make a difference. He wanted to build the kind of company he had always wanted to be a part of, an organization based on the golden rule. "Our vision was to create a bank that would be known for how it loved its team members, loved its customers, and loved the communities it was a part of," said Casey. As part of his focus on loving others, Casey also made another decision. If the company became wildly successful, he would put a limit on his personal income and direct the excess profits toward helping people.

He and associate Toby Harris decided to call the company Movement Mortgage, and they started it in 2008, just as the Great Recession started. "Banks were known for how they had drained life from communities by issuing bad loans where defaults would become almost inevitable," said Casey. "Entire communities collapsed under the weight of excessive mortgage debt tanking the value of all the homes in the communities."

"I had a vision to tell a new and better story of how a business and more particularly a bank could be used powerfully as an agent of change for good," said Casey. While large banks struggled to comply with new regulations such as the Dodd-Frank Act, Casey's company innovated and kept its focus on helping clients. Movement Mortgage instituted what they called their 6–7–1 policy. That was a promise to underwrite a loan within six hours of application, process a qualified borrower's documents in seven days, and attempt to close the loan in one day. Most of their customers closed in fewer than thirty days. That was quite a contrast with the normal loan processing time of forty-five, sixty, or ninety days.[24]

The success of Movement Mortgage has been extraordinary. It started with four employees. Twelve years later, it employs more than four thousand. They have offices in nearly eight hundred locations across forty-seven states.[25] The company processed more than $16 billion in loans in 2019 and ranked in the top ten in the nation in retail lending.[26] But those numbers aren't what excites Casey. Changing the lives of people does.

He does that by providing good mortgages to people who might not otherwise be able to get one, but it doesn't stop there. He also does it by helping his employees. That started when the company began quietly helping team members in times of financial crisis. When they learned a single mom was living in her car, they helped her find a place to live. They helped victims of domestic abuse. They supported employees who were struggling financially to keep them from being evicted.

That was relatively easy when they had few employees. With the growth of the company, the challenge has become more difficult and complex. In response, Casey launched the Love Works Fund within Movement Mortgage to continue financial support to Movement's employees and their family members in times of crisis. So far, the company has given $3.4 million to its employees! Casey estimates that 70 percent of the company's employees give to the fund. Movement Mortgage matches their contribution.

COMMUNITY TEAMWORK

As rewarding as it is to help his company's customers and employees, that wasn't enough for Casey. Remembering his childhood experiences in the depressed areas of Washington, DC, he wanted to help people in struggling communities in Charlotte, and he believed the best way to do that would be by offering better educational opportunities for local children. He created the Movement Foundation and began researching charter schools. He found a model that worked, and in 2017, Movement School, a free charter school, opened in an underserved community in Charlotte. It began with a kindergarten and first and second grades, with a plan to add a grade each year, up through eighth grade. It was so successful that two years after it opened, the waiting list of children who wanted to enroll was almost double the school's student population.

Casey quickly began looking for ways to open additional schools. But something else happened as a result of the school's success. A local hospital system informed Casey that healthcare was a challenge for people in the area because there wasn't one pediatrician within five miles of the school. In response, Casey and his team arranged to offer space in a nearby community center so they could open an urban health clinic.

A few months later Casey and his team were approached by a nonprofit developer who wanted to address the affordable housing crisis in the area. Casey and the developer put together a team, worked with a generous landowner in town, and received a charitable gift from a church, making it possible to build 185 affordable housing units between the school and the health clinic. And other opportunities for Casey and Movement Mortgage to make a difference keep coming. So far, the Movement Foundation has invested $40 million of company profits in projects dedicated to making a positive difference in the world.[27]

"What started as a vision to bring a transformative school to a challenged area of our city turned into a holistic redemptive development," said Casey. "As a person who has always loved being on teams and appreciated the power of teamwork, there is something powerful about seeing a community come together."

"Problems in America are too large for any organization to tackle alone," said Casey. "Hospitals alone cannot change the experience of the urban poor. Schools alone will not change this. Housing alone will not solve the myriad problems that exist today for our children born into poverty. But great organizations working together with the right leadership for these types of teams makes me hopeful about what can be done to love some of the most vulnerable children in society today." In other words, we all need one another.

THE NEED FOR ONE ANOTHER IS EVERYWHERE

Author and speaker Patricia Fripp said, "A team is not just people who work at the same time in the same place. A real team is a group of very different individuals who share a commitment to working together to achieve common goals. Most likely they are not all equal in experience, talent, or education, but they are equal in one vitally important way: their commitment to the good of the organization. Any group of people—your family, your workplace, or your community—gets the best results by working as a team."[28] If we work together, we can win together, making a difference.

As Rob and I began writing this chapter, we knew the ideas

we were presenting applied to every person working to change any aspect of their world—great or small. But you can see the same need for everyone's effort on a small scale in everyday events today: a soccer match, a basketball game, or a football game. If one person is missing or isn't adequately fulfilling his or her role, the team loses. At work, if you're involved in a project, and a team member isn't pulling his weight, the job becomes much harder for everyone else. At home, when a family member doesn't do his part, everyone in the family suffers.

Teamwork is essential and makes everyone's efforts stronger, whether the project or objective is large or small. What does it take to be an effective team? Julie Lambert said it requires the following:

Tolerance of each other's weaknesses.
Encouragement towards each other's successes.
Acknowledgment that each of us has something to offer.
Mindfulness that all of us appreciate those three qualities.

The scope of the project matters little. The cause can be anything worthwhile. When individuals put the team ahead of themselves, when they share the same values, when they collaborate together using whatever assets they possess for their cause, they can make a huge difference.

> IF YOU WANT TO CHANGE YOUR WORLD IN A BIG WAY, THEN YOU KNOW WHAT YOU NEED TO DO: TEAM UP!

If you want to change your world in a big way, then you know what you need to do: team up!

CHAPTER 4

LET'S ALL
GET ON THE
SAME PAGE

If you want to go fast, go alone. If you want to go far, go together.

—AFRICAN PROVERB

When Rob and I sat down to begin writing *Change Your World*, we had two purposes in mind. First, we wanted to motivate and equip you to make a difference *right now* in your community. Second, we wanted to encourage you to change your community *with* others. When this happens, there is potential for a movement to be birthed. And that's a very good thing. Movements bring awareness to problems. Injustices mobilize leadership and inspire people to action. All those things create positive momentum for change. Movements, whether mini or maxi, can change the world.

WHY PEOPLE RALLY
AROUND A CAUSE

In the previous chapter, we wrote about how people working together *always* accomplish more than individuals who labor alone. When they come together and create a movement, it can be powerful. Why does that happen?

THEY ARE SEEKING CONNECTION WITH OTHERS

People seek out connection with others in many ways and places. They go to bars. They go to gyms. They join clubs, sports teams, and fantasy football leagues. They desire a sense of community, which begins with people getting together. People often seek out other people based on a shared sense of purpose. People who possess this desire for accomplishment don't want to get together just for the sake of getting together. They want more. That shared sense of purpose creates an extra level of connection that can lead to the making of a movement.

THEY WANT TO BE PART OF SOMETHING BIGGER THAN THEMSELVES

Human beings are always searching for meaning. Busyness is not satisfying. A life of purpose is. It can be deeply satisfying to be part of something larger than yourself. Most people are looking for a way to be involved in something they're passionate about that they can do with other like-minded people. They want to be a part of a story that allows them to express their deepest desires and highest aspirations. They want to create memories doing something memorable. Why else would people wear colored bracelets identifying a cause, dress in pink during Breast Cancer

Awareness Month, get doused for the Ice-Bucket Challenge, or give to organizations they believe in? When enough people who share the same values follow their desires to make a difference and join to do it together, a movement is born.

THEY WANT TO RECEIVE VALUE FROM GIVING

There is another reason people rally around a cause, but this is the part people rarely talk about. We want to think that when others join a cause, it's because the cause is compelling, important, and justified. While it's true that these are the motivation for some, most people desire a personal return on their time and effort. That immediate return is often how good we feel for wanting to add value to others. This is the start of the significance journey. We give. And the longer we stay on this giving path, the more we realize that helping others helps us.

> THE INEVITABLE RETURN: GIVE TO OTHERS LONG ENOUGH, AND WE RECEIVE MORE THAN WE GIVE. LOVE PEOPLE DEEPLY ENOUGH, AND LOVE RETURNS TO US TENFOLD. LIFT PEOPLE UP, AND WE GET LIFTED EVEN HIGHER.

I call this process the Inevitable Return. Give to others long enough, and we receive more than we give. Love people deeply enough, and love returns to us tenfold. Lift people up, and we get lifted even higher.

The Inevitable Return of adding value to others occurs in steps. Look at the ones we've listed below and try to identify where you are right now:

Step	Significant Statement
Desire	"I want to add value to others."
Question	"How can I add value to others?"
Community	"I know people who add value to others."
Observation	"I see how they add value to others."
Joining	"Can I help you add value to others?"
Equipping	"I know how to add value to others."
Action	"I am adding value to others!"
Feedback	"They tell me I'm adding value to them."
Fulfillment	"I am content when I'm adding value to others."
Motivation	"I want to keep adding value to others."
Sharing	"Let's add value to one other."
Growing	"Let's find others to add value to."
Changing	"Adding value to others is changing me."
Receiving	"Those who I added value to have multiplied value back to me!"

What are the results of taking these steps of significance? The Inevitable Return! Here's what Rob and I know: keep walking forward by adding value to people, and the personal return will increase with each step.

People want to join a movement that includes connecting with others and being part of a community doing something bigger than themselves. And they are rewarded for their efforts by gaining personal identity and recognition. Rob and I desire that for you. We want *Change Your World* to be a resource that helps you become part of a transformational movement. For this to happen, we all need to get on the same page. Let's all be part of the movement to make a difference.

WHY SOME ATTEMPTS AT MOVEMENT DON'T MOVE

Rob and I have worked for decades to try to facilitate transformational movements. Rob has worked with children and youth in nearly every country in the world for more than thirty years. For forty years I've trained leaders around the world, and for the last decade I've gone to developing countries to train people to lead transformational roundtables. In addition, Rob has also studied movements, both as an invested leader and as an academic.

In the process, we've learned some things about transformation—what works and what doesn't. We want to acquaint you with what we've observed to help you be successful, whether you're trying to lead a movement or join one. Let's start by taking a look at why many attempted movements fail.

LACK OF UNITY

Do you remember the Occupy Wall Street movement? It was big news a decade ago but no longer exists. It started on September 17, 2011, when two hundred people gathered in Zuccotti Park in New York City's financial district and camped out in tents there for almost a month to protest income inequality. The catalyst for the gathering was a poster with the message: "What is our one demand? Occupy Wall Street. Bring tent."[1] In response, people showed up.

If "occupying" was their goal, then you could say they achieved it. But what were they really trying to achieve? That's difficult to say. They came to the same location, but they didn't unite around the same cause. Some of the issues Occupy Wall Street wanted to address were the following:

- Income inequality
- The need for a higher minimum wage
- Protest against the Keystone XL Pipeline
- Climate change
- Anti-fracking
- Corporate influence on politics
- The student debt crisis[2]

According to the *Atlantic* magazine, "Occupy was, at its core, a movement constrained by its own contradictions: filled with leaders who declared themselves leaderless, governed by a consensus-based structure that failed to reach consensus, and seeking to transform politics while refusing to become political."[3] No wonder Occupy fizzled into nothing.

ABSENCE OF A POSITIVE GOAL

It's difficult to create a focused agenda and build a movement when you're *against* something instead of *for* something. That was another downfall of Occupy Wall Street. People who participated in that brief movement were very vocal about the many things they were against, but they had no clear positive message about what they were for.

Why is not having a positive goal a problem? Venting doesn't create transformation. You can't build a transformative process based on what you don't like. Negative emotion often comes first when we see injustice or

> IT'S DIFFICULT TO CREATE A FOCUSED AGENDA AND BUILD A MOVEMENT WHEN YOU'RE *AGAINST* SOMETHING INSTEAD OF *FOR* SOMETHING.

tragedy, and that negative emotion is often the strongest emotion we feel, but it's not long-lasting. And it's not particularly healthy to try to sustain negative emotion. Besides, being against something isn't attractive. It doesn't draw positive people who want to work for positive change. If you want to create positive change in the world, you have to be *for* something.

INADEQUATE LEADERSHIP

When we see a problem or injustice, author Seth Godin said, "The easiest thing is to react. The second easiest thing is to respond. But the hardest thing is to initiate."[4] Yet that is what transformational leaders need to do. They need to initiate. That is the first step in changing the world for good.

> "THE EASIEST THING IS TO REACT. THE SECOND EASIEST THING IS TO RESPOND. BUT THE HARDEST THING IS TO INITIATE."
> —SETH GODIN

One of the greatest movements for good of the twentieth century was for civil rights for African Americans in the United States. The leader of that movement was Martin Luther King Jr. He came to national prominence when he was asked to lead a bus boycott in Montgomery, Alabama, in 1955 and 1956 because of his background, professional standing, and leadership. The boycott is considered to have been the first large-scale demonstration against segregation in the United States. By the time the boycott ended, the Supreme Court ruled that segregation on public transportation was illegal.[5]

After the success of the boycott, in early 1957 King and sixty other ministers and civil rights leaders formed the Southern Christian Leadership Conference (SCLC), with King selected as the organization's president.[6] The SCLC, drawing on a philosophy of Christian nonviolence, framed civil rights as a moral issue. With King leading, the organization coordinated mass nonviolent protest campaigns, voter registration drives, and the March on Washington for Jobs and Freedom, which was estimated to have drawn 250,000 people.[7] And it helped precipitate passage of the Civil Rights Act of 1964 and the Voting Rights Act of 1965.[8] For his efforts, King received the Nobel Peace Prize. At age thirty-five, he was, at that time, its youngest recipient.[9]

In 1968, as the civil rights movement was gaining momentum, King was assassinated. His close friend and SCLC vice president Ralph David Abernathy succeeded him, but the movement was never the same again. Nobody has been able to step into King's leadership shoes since his death. They may be able to receive his old title, but they can't lead and champion the cause the way he did. The lesson is that transformational movements aren't successful and sustainable unless they are led by transformational leaders. Like everything else, they rise and fall on leadership.

I want to give you one final thought about leadership. Great leaders like Martin Luther King Jr. didn't start out as great leaders. In fact, King didn't elevate himself to be the leader of the movement. Others did. He was part of a small group who wanted to do something about racial injustice in America. When he got started, he and his friends simply did what they *could* where they *were*. From there, they continued to take steps forward. The lesson

> TRANSFORMATIONAL MOVEMENTS AREN'T SUCCESSFUL AND SUSTAINABLE UNLESS THEY ARE LED BY TRANSFORMATIONAL LEADERS.

is that great leaders who make a difference are not born that way. They are formed into great leaders as they move with others to make a difference for those around them.

LACK OF ORGANIZATIONAL SUPPORT

At some point, for a movement to be sustainable, it needs people who will support it organizationally. Otherwise it will die out. But that doesn't mean it needs to be a single formal organization in a traditional sense. It just needs to comprise people who are dedicated to helping all the players who are involved. Whether the support comes from a single leader, a group of volunteers, or a formal organization with paid employees, it fulfills the same function. It helps the people fighting for the cause to work together, communicate, and be more effective. They become the backbone of the movement.

THINKING MONEY IS THE ANSWER

There's one other roadblock that can keep a potential movement from moving forward. It's believing, *If we just had the money*, our problem would be solved. While it is true that there are some things you can do only if you have the resources, it's not true that money solves every problem. For example, the World Bank's Independent Evaluation Group found that in twenty-five poor countries in which they invested in the mid-1990s to the early 2000s, half of the countries had the same or worse poverty rates than they had before billions of dollars in aid had been spent there.[10]

Money will not automatically create a movement. Transformation can't be bought. Movements have begun without a penny being spent. And wealthy people have spent millions trying to make something happen with no results. Think about billionaire

Michael Bloomberg's campaign during the 2020 presidential primary. He spent nearly a billion dollars on his campaign.[11] That was more than all the other Democratic candidates still in the race combined.[12] For all that spending, he won one primary: American Samoa.[13]

> **MONEY WILL NOT AUTOMATICALLY CREATE A MOVEMENT. TRANSFORMATION CAN'T BE BOUGHT.**

Bloomberg lacked a grassroots group of people who believed in his vision, strategy, and ability to transform the nation. If a large group of people who believed in him had been on the ground supporting his leadership, his money would have been a useful tool to help his campaign. But because Bloomberg wasn't backed by a movement, he tried to pay for one. In the end, he did the only thing he could do: drop out of the race.

HOW TRANSFORMATION HAPPENS

What, then, causes movements to move? How does transformation occur? What are the keys to change? We want to show you five pictures that illustrate how transformational movements happen:

A WATERFALL: TOP-DOWN—IT REQUIRES LEADERSHIP

Transformation begins with influence, and influence always flows from the top down, like a waterfall, not upward. For transformation to happen, the leaders must be involved. In the John Maxwell Company's corporate training division, we saw this truth play out time after time. When an organization engaged our team to train their employees, the number-one indicator of whether the training would work was the level of involvement by the leaders. If the leaders of the organization *sent* their teams to the training, the results were uneven and unremarkable. If the leaders *joined* their teams in the training, the results were consistent and positive. To have any chance of significant transformation, the leaders must give their voice, approval, influence, and involvement to the movement.

> TRANSFORMATION BEGINS WITH INFLUENCE, AND INFLUENCE ALWAYS FLOWS FROM THE TOP DOWN, LIKE A WATERFALL, NOT UPWARD.

Rob began leading OneHope during the time of *glasnost* and *perestroika* with the Soviet Union, when the USSR was on the cusp of failing. At that time, the Soviet minister of education reached out to Rob's organization and asked to meet with him. He and other leaders in the country were worried. He wanted to know about the values Rob's team was teaching children around the world using *Book of Hope*, which OneHope published. He told Rob, "Something new is coming to our country, and it is called 'choice.' And with choice, will come everything from the West. Movies, music, drugs, and pornography—we may become the greatest moral catastrophe this world has ever seen! If what you are telling me is true and this book can bring hope and answers to our children, we welcome you into our nation."

Rob left that meeting with a letter allowing OneHope to give the *Book of Hope* to fifty-eight million children, that is, every pupil in the Soviet Union. How was that possible? The minister of education had done his homework by studying OneHope, which had gained credibility under the leadership of Rob's father, Bob. OneHope had worked in El Salvador with its minister of education, then in Chile under President Augusto Pinochet, and in Nicaragua when it was led by Daniel Ortega. OneHope's efforts had helped children in other contexts, which made the USSR's minister of education believe it could work there. That leader's permission from the top empowered Rob to take action. Without it, OneHope would never have been able to do *anything* in the USSR. That just goes to show you: when leaders use their influence to get behind something, they can make things happen.

When the John Maxwell Leadership Foundation (JMLF) began teaching values in Guatemala and seeing positive results throughout the country, people in other nations began contacting us and asking us to start similar initiatives in their countries. While we are always open to the prospect of going to new countries, we know that our efforts will have a chance to make a difference only if the top leaders in the country have bought into the idea. So far, in addition to Guatemala, we've started teaching values through transformational roundtables in Paraguay and Costa Rica because the presidents of those countries invited us.

We also were contacted by G. T. Bustin, who leads two international charities in Papua New Guinea. He has a passion to serve his nation, and when he learned what we were doing in Latin America, he asked us to come to New Guinea to teach values in roundtables. Two of my nonprofit leaders, George Hoskins and John Vereecken, traveled to New Guinea to meet G. T. While there, they met a leader who told them he was sick and tired of being sick and tired of the corruption in his country.

George and John saw that G. T. was a man of integrity who sincerely wanted to change his world. The need for change was evident, and the possibilities were great. But for us to go there, the country's leaders needed to be on board and involved, and George and John told him that. A quiet influencer, G. T. began connecting with leaders in business and government in New Guinea. Several months later, we received a message from the nation's prime minister, inviting us to come to his country to start the process.

When we launch transformation tables in New Guinea, hopefully in 2021, we will do the same thing we do when we accept the invitation to any country. We will make contact with high-level leaders in each of the eight streams of influence there and ask for their commitment to be an ongoing part of the process. Only when they get involved and lend their voices and influence to the initiative will we launch it.

Influence flows down, not up. Leadership buy-in at the top of the waterfall allows our transformational efforts to cascade down into the eight streams of influence and then throughout the country.

A LADDER: BOTTOM-UP—IT ENCOURAGES MOBILITY

While influence flows down, transformation climbs up. That's why we associate it with the image of a ladder. When you help people to improve their lives, they rise up. They begin to dream of a better world, which is fantastic, because the only tragedy greater than dying with dreams unfulfilled is never to have dreamed at all.

In 1931 the phrase *the American dream* was coined by James Truslow Adams in his book *The Epic of America*. During the Great Depression, he saw the great promise of the United States, where people could rise up and pursue their potential without many of the societal or economic barriers people in other parts of the world had battled for generations. Adams wrote:

> The *American dream* [is] that dream of a land in which life should be better and richer and fuller for every man, with opportunity for each according to ability or achievement. It is a difficult dream for the European upper classes to interpret adequately, and too many of us ourselves have grown weary and mistrustful of it. It is not a dream of motor cars and high wages merely, but a dream of social order in which each man and each woman shall be able to attain to the fullest stature of which they are innately capable, and be recognized by others for what they are, regardless of the fortuitous circumstances of birth or position.[14]

We believe what has been called the American Dream could become every country's dream because everyone desires to reach their potential and live a better life. But there must be a ladder available to them. Does the ladder create the dream? Does the dream create the ladder? The answer may be both—as long as there is hope. When you have hope, the words of Nido Qubein, the president of High Point University, ring true: "Your present circumstances don't determine where you can go; they merely determine where you start."

When people are encouraged to dream, assisted in improving themselves through good values, and empowered

> "YOUR PRESENT CIRCUMSTANCES DON'T DETERMINE WHERE YOU CAN GO; THEY MERELY DETERMINE WHERE YOU START."
> —NIDO QUBEIN

to climb the ladder of success, they can also begin to make things better for others. They can transition from survival thinking, which asks, "How can I make it through the day?" to significance thinking, which asks, "How can I make someone else's day?"

We saw this shift from survival thinking to significant thinking play out during the coronavirus disease (COVID-19) pandemic in 2020:

- Teachers offered their classes online.
- Neighbors shared necessities like food, water, and toilet paper.
- Stores offered special hours to elderly and medically fragile people.
- Restaurants offered free delivery.
- Neighbors sang to one another from balconies in Italy.
- People donated large amounts of cash to stock food banks.
- Employers found ways to continue paying wages after the workplace had been shut down.
- Neighborhoods put up Christmas lights to boost spirits.
- Musicians performed online concerts.
- People bought gift cards from small businesses to keep them afloat.

There was a generosity of spirit among humankind.

This kind of positive, unselfish spirit was what Martin Luther King Jr. was describing when he said:

A true revolution of values will soon cause us to question the fairness and justice of many of our past and present policies. On the one hand we are called to play the Good Samaritan on life's roadside, but that will be only an initial act. One day we must come to see that the whole Jericho Road must be transformed so that men and women will not be constantly beaten and robbed as they make their journey on life's highway. True compassion is more than flinging a coin to a beggar. It comes to see that an edifice which produces beggars needs restructuring.[15]

Qubein said, "Transformational movements that value people and add value to them can rebuild our world." As the JMLF began helping people learn and live good values, they became more capable. They developed greater self-respect and self-awareness. They were better workers, spouses, parents, and citizens. Their lives improved, and they began helping others to improve their lives.

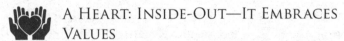 A HEART: INSIDE-OUT—IT EMBRACES VALUES

Businessman Bill McDermott said, "Every movement has a single point of origin." That origin is always in the heart of a person. It is an expression of the heart, birthed in the values that person has embraced, and from there it flows outward and manifests itself in the individual's behaviors and communication. From there, it can spread to others.

When the JMLF got ready to launch its transformational values roundtable initiative in Guatemala, head trainers Dawn Yoder and Mike Poulin were searching for a way to succinctly communicate the spirit of what we were trying to do to the more than two hundred volunteer trainers who had flown to Guatemala to go out and train roundtable facilitators. The ultimate goal was to see the transformation of the country as its people learned and lived good values. That may seem like a lofty goal. How could it become a reality? It began with the facilitators learning and living out good values themselves as they encouraged the people at their transformation tables to do it. Living good values precedes giving good values. Because people do what people see, the facilitators had to be examples of the values they shared. Transformation is more than a lesson to be learned; it is a life to be lived. That doesn't happen when it's imposed from the outside. It happens from the inside when people embrace values in the heart. To communicate this transformational truth, Dawn and Mike kept repeating one phrase as we introduced transformation tables to those volunteers: "*La transformación está en mí*" (transformation is in me).

Every person has the potential to experience transformation, and each person who became part of a transformation table needed to understand two things. First, they needed to see value in themselves before they could see the value in helping others transform. And second, they had to recognize that the only thing standing between them and a better life was their willingness to live good values. As Mahatma Gandhi is reputed to have said, "Your values become your destiny." If each person sees to his own transformation, and enough people do the same, the company or organization, the community, and the country will change.

JOINED HANDS: SIDE BY SIDE—IT DESIRES PARTNERSHIPS

The Law of Mount Everest in *The 17 Indisputable Laws of Teamwork* says, "As the challenge escalates, the need for teamwork elevates." Transformation of any community is a Mount Everest type of challenge, which means it requires many people working together. That means engaging in partnerships.

As I have worked to lead transformational efforts in places around the world, my organizations have always focused on using partnerships. Sometimes we've succeeded, and sometimes we haven't, but we've learned a lot in both cases. When the JMLF begins working to bring transformation into a country, we always work with well-led local organizations who want to change their world. They help us to connect and partner with leaders in the eight streams of influence, which we stated are government, education, business, religion, media, arts, sports, and health care. The leaders from those areas come together to form a cabinet. Together, they identify their nation's most pressing needs and what can be done to make the country better and brighter.

> AS THE CHALLENGE ESCALATES, THE NEED FOR TEAMWORK ELEVATES.

The challenges vary from region to region, based on their unique needs and culture. In Guatemala, the JMLF made a commitment to teach values to children in school for 180 days a year. In Papua New Guinea, leaders wanted to work to end gender-based violence. Whatever the goals, the JMLF offers its influence, resources, and tools to help leaders in these eight streams. As these leaders are changed, they begin to have a transformational impact on the people around them.

As individuals embrace good values, they realize they have the potential to change their own lives. They begin to realize they have the opportunity to add value to others. And transformation begins to spread and to produce lasting positive change at a personal level, then a community level, and ultimately a national level.

The bottom line is that transformation begins in an individual, grows in community, and impacts a society. But the process always starts with partnerships based on common ground. That's possible even when people come from completely different backgrounds and cultures. An extraordinary example can be found in a story Rob tells about William Carey, an English missionary and educator who moved to India in 1793 and remained there until his death in 1834. A few years after establishing himself in India, he witnessed *sati*, the ceremonial death by burning of a widow on the funeral pyre of her recently deceased husband.

The horrific practice of widows burning themselves to death was deeply entrenched in parts of India. The earliest Western records indicate that action had been occurring for at least two thousand years.[16] The term *sati* means "virtuous wife," and the practice of sacrifice was believed to be holy.

From the first time Carey witnessed sati, when he unsuccessfully begged the widow not to allow herself to be burned to death, he worked relentlessly to stop this practice that devalued women in such a brutal way. Carey connected with influential Indian leaders and worked with them to get sati outlawed. He was able to form a partnership with Hindu religious and social reformer Raja Ram Mohan Roy. Their common ground was the agreement that all people had value. Together they persuaded Governor Lord William Bentinck to make the practice illegal.[17] Sati was finally banned in 1829.

If people from two distant parts of the world, from two vastly different cultures, embracing two starkly different religions could find common ground to partner together, then we can feel confident that we can connect with anyone if we're willing to give it a try.

In the book *Power of 2*, Rodd Wagner and Gale Muller write about partnerships and how important they are to achievement. Relying on research by Gallup, they found eight elements of a powerful partnership, to which Rob and I added two others:

- Complementary strengths
- A common mission
- Fairness
- Trust
- Acceptance
- Forgiveness
- Communicating
- Unselfishness[18]
- Time
- Valuing the partner's contribution

As you prepare to join hands with others to try to change your world, look for these common values to increase your odds of success.

We'll say one more thing about this. I'm sure you noticed that a common mission was near the top of the list for Wagner and Muller. What's interesting is that while partners must be in agreement on the mission, they don't need to have common motives for trying to achieve it. They write:

> Although you and your collaborator must agree on your mission, you don't have to have the same reasons for pursuing it. Successful partnerships often have different motivations for making the climb. This usually does not hinder the alliance, particularly if both of you understand the driving force motivating the other and work to see those hopes fulfilled.[19]

However, without that common mission, partners tend to drift toward their own individual pursuits.

A TABLE: FEW TO MANY—IT ENABLES GROWTH

The birth of transformation starts in the heart of an individual, and the growth of the movement happens around a table. Mass movements don't begin with the masses. They begin with a few people. When people can sit around the table together as equal contributors, everyone wins.

We've only recently begun using transformation tables in Costa Rica, but already we're hearing stories of growth. One of those stories came from Juanita García. She and her family moved to Costa Rica from Nicaragua to seek a better life. She dreamed of furthering her education but had to drop out of elementary school so she could work to help her family. As a teenager, she became a mother and lost hope for bettering her life.

But then she came into contact with an organization that helped young women in her situation. It was there she joined one of our transformation tables. She said, "I experienced the greatest change of my life because I discovered that my story could change if I anticipated opportunities." Citing what she learned from applying the value *initiative* to her life, she enrolled in night school and completed her education. Her success inspired her husband to enroll in technical school. And her son, Matías, became a better student in school as well. Her success also inspired her to become trained to facilitate transformation tables. "I did it to help other women in my community with stories like mine so that they can have the opportunity to have a new way of life, a life of transformation."

> MASS MOVEMENTS DON'T BEGIN WITH THE MASSES. THEY BEGIN WITH A FEW PEOPLE.

This concept of transformation tables is so important to changing your world that Rob and I have dedicated an entire chapter to it, so we won't give you the details here. We'll just say that transformation tables provide a safe place to sit, learn, and share good values. From there they can spread, providing a place for everyone to become part of the movement.

A BRIDGE: HERE TO THERE—IT LEADS TO TRANSFORMATION

The ultimate goal of any movement is to create a better future. It starts with good values. Good values create growth. Growth creates transformation. Transformation creates movement. Movement creates change. And change helps us cross over into a better future. Each of these stages, together, forms a bridge from here to there. Crossing the bridge and taking that journey from here to there becomes a great story, one worth telling. As people share it, others want to join and become part of the story. That inspires them to grow, and as they do, the entire cycle continues.

When we think of the word *transformation* or hear the word *movement*, we sometimes imagine that it has to be big. But sometimes small actions lead to big differences in a community of people. For example, a small school in the rural countryside of Paraguay was experiencing conflict among the teachers and with the school's principal. The communication between them was strained at best, and there was no sense of collaboration. However, that school was one in which the iLead program was being introduced. The faculty were entrusted with the task of overseeing the students as they facilitated transformation tables. As part of the program, the teachers were also given an opportunity to interact with one another to discuss how the program was going and what the students were learning. To their surprise, their discussions opened up the lines of communication between the teachers. That inspired them to communicate better with the principal. And as a result, everyone became more collaborative. Together, they had built a bridge that allowed the entire school to transform.

As you think about these six pictures—a waterfall, a ladder, a heart, joined hands, a table, and a bridge—can you see yourself in one or more of them? We hope you do. Because you must be moved if you want become part of a movement greater than yourself. We hope these pictures inspire you to change and grow.

Which picture do you most identify with? Which resonates with you most strongly? Perhaps that may reveal your primary role in a transformational movement. More important, you understand how a transformational movement works.

In this chapter and the previous ones, the subject of values has come up a number of times. There's a reason for that. You cannot make a difference or change your world in a positive way unless you build everything you do on good values. They are the single most important part of any transformational movement. And that's why we've dedicated the entire next chapter to the value of values.

CHAPTER 5

EXPERIENCE THE VALUE OF VALUES

Vision and mission are the head and the heart of people. But values are their soul.

Shortly after the Enron scandal in the early 2000s, I was having dinner with Larry Kirshbaum, who was then the CEO of the Time Warner Book Group. We started talking about the erosion of values, and Larry asked me if I would write a book on business ethics for corporate America.

Immediately I knew I had a challenge. Good business ethics are the result of knowing and living good values. I wondered if there was a value that could be embraced by all people, regardless of culture or religion? I needed to identify a value that could be a foundation for all human conduct. After a few weeks of thinking and researching, I was convinced the golden rule was that foundational value and that people everywhere could build an ethical life on it. After all, I had discovered that the golden rule was part of nearly every culture and religion. Here are examples:

- **Christianity:** "Do to others whatever you would like them to do to you."[1]
- **Islam:** "None of you has faith until he loves for his brother or his neighbor what he loves for himself."[2]
- **Judaism:** "What is hateful to you, do not do to your fellow man. This is the entire Law; all the rest is commentary."[3]
- **Buddhism:** "Hurt not others in ways that you yourself would find hurtful."[4]
- **Hinduism:** "This is the sum of duty; do naught unto others what you would not have them do unto you."[5]
- **Zoroastrianism:** "Whatever is disagreeable to yourself do not do unto others."[6]
- **Confucianism:** "Do not do unto others what you would not have them do to you."[7]
- **Bahai:** "And if thine eyes be turned towards justice, choose thou for thy neighbour that which thou choosest for thyself."[8]
- **Jainism:** "A man should wander about treating all creatures as he himself would be treated."[9]
- **Yoruba Proverb (Nigeria):** "One going to take a pointed stick to pinch a baby bird should first try it on himself to feel how it hurts."[10]

So I agreed to write Ethics 101. And since that time, I have committed to teaching values for the rest of my life.

A CASE FOR GOOD VALUES

I'm known for stating that everything rises and falls on leadership. But do you know what two things are responsible for making leadership rise? The first is *competence*. No one wants to follow an incompetent leader. The second is *values*. Values are principles that guide your decisions and behaviors. When those values are good, they bring only benefits—never harm—to yourself and others. When leaders have good values, which are reflected in their behaviors, people are willing to trust and to follow them. Good values allow leaders and everyone else to help others.

> VALUES ARE PRINCIPLES THAT GUIDE YOUR DECISIONS AND BEHAVIORS. WHEN THOSE VALUES ARE GOOD, THEY BRING ONLY BENEFITS— NEVER HARM—TO YOURSELF AND OTHERS.

Recently I was reading *The Infinite Game* by Simon Sinek, where he discusses the difference between a just cause and a person's *why*. He says that a just cause is a specific vision of a future state that does not yet exist, a future state so appealing that people are willing to make sacrifices in order to help advance that vision. He contrasts that with a *why*. He wrote:

A WHY comes from the past. It is an origin story. It is a statement of who we are—the sum total of our values and beliefs. A Just Cause is about the future. It defines where we are going. It describes a world we hope to live in and will commit to help build. Everyone has their own WHY (and everyone can know what their WHY is if they choose to uncover it). But we do not have to have our own Just Cause, we can choose to join someone else's. Indeed we can start a movement, or we can choose to join one and make it our own. . . .

Think of the WHY like the foundation of a house, it is the starting point. It gives whatever we build upon it strength and permanence. Our Just Cause is the ideal vision of the house we hope to build. We can work a lifetime to build it and still we will not be finished. However, the results of our work help give the house form. As it moves from our imagination to reality it inspires more people to join the Cause and continue the work . . . forever.[11]

"A JUST CAUSE IS ABOUT THE FUTURE. IT DEFINES WHERE WE ARE GOING. IT DESCRIBES A WORLD WE HOPE TO LIVE IN AND WILL COMMIT TO HELP BUILD."
—SIMON SINEK

Transformation is a just cause worthy of commitment. Rob and I are giving our best for it. My just cause is to equip people to learn and live good values that increase their value to themselves and others. What just cause are you working toward? What is your vision of a better future? Sinek said a just cause must meet five criteria:

- For something—affirmative and optimistic
- Inclusive—open to all those who would like to contribute
- Service oriented—for the primary benefit of others
- Resilient—able to endure political, technological and culture change
- Idealistic—big, bold, and ultimately unachievable[12]

I would add that it must be based on good values. Many years ago James Dobson analyzed the disillusionment many people experience between the ages of thirty-five and fifty. It's often called a midlife crisis. Dobson's observation was that people become disillusioned when they discover they have been living by the wrong value system. He described it this way: "All of a sudden you realize the ladder you've been climbing is leaning against the wrong wall."[13] If we want to change our world, we can't just climb the ladder of success. We need to climb the ladder of good values.

> IF WE WANT TO CHANGE OUR WORLD, WE CAN'T JUST CLIMB THE LADDER OF SUCCESS. WE NEED TO CLIMB THE LADDER OF GOOD VALUES.

THE VALUE OF GOOD VALUES

I think most people would agree that good values are important, but at the same time they'd rather move on to discuss strategy for changing the world. It's almost as though they take values for granted, assuming that people will learn and embrace good values on their own. But *being* has to precede *doing* if you want to change your world. That's why we want to spend this entire chapter discussing good values and how to help others embrace them. Nothing impacts your life every day more than your values.

GOOD VALUES MAKE POSITIVE CHANGE POSSIBLE

Many of our personal characteristics are a matter of birth. We were born with certain talents and abilities and certain deficits.

When I was a kid, I loved to play basketball, but I was never going to be good enough to become a pro. It just wasn't in me. Similarly, you could threaten me, even insist that I become a ballet dancer *or else*, but you'd have to follow through on the "or else." It doesn't matter how hard I might try; it's never going to happen.

That's not true when it comes to values. No matter where or when you were born, no matter how much or how little talent or intelligence you possess, no matter the circumstances of your upbringing, you can learn, embrace, and practice good values. It's your choice.

When the John Maxwell Leadership Foundation starts a transformation initiative in a country, one of the first things representatives from the foundation do is ask people from the eight streams of influence in that country (government, business, arts, education, faith, media, sports, and health care) to choose the values they most want to see taught to people. To simplify the process, we provide a list from which they can choose:

Attitude	Gratitude	Listening	Responsibility
Commitment	Hope	Love	Self-Regulation
Communication	Humility	Perseverance	Self-Worth
Courage	Initiative	Personal Growth	Servanthood
Fairness	Integrity	Priorities	Teachability
Forgiveness	Kindness	Relationships	Teamwork
Generosity	Leadership	Respect	Work Ethic

Take a moment and look at these values. Which of them you would like to apply to your life to improve it? The good news is that all of them are within your reach. Why? Because each value is attainable if you choose to work on it. Regardless of your education, intelligence, gifting, or skills, you can live any or all of those values. You can choose to do it. Choice is the difference maker when it comes to values. Choosing makes change possible.

One of the most remarkable stories of choices based on good values came to us from Mexico. A business owner in Chihuahua decided to lead transformation tables with his employees using the values curriculum created by the JMLF. The day they talked about the value of forgiveness, the owner, who was leading the discussion, sensed something was different from their previous sessions. That difference became clear when Rene, one of his employees, said, "Forgiveness sounds really good, and I'm willing to apply it to my life—except for one specific area." He went on to explain that his brother had been murdered many years before. He knew who had done it, that his brother had pleaded for his life, and the man had shown no mercy. Rene had been actively searching for the killer for ten years. "Once I find him," he said, "I will get my revenge. I'll kill him. That's the only way to wipe away the pain and make things right."

> CHOICE IS THE DIFFERENCE MAKER WHEN IT COMES TO VALUES. CHOOSING MAKES CHANGE POSSIBLE.

The owner was horrified and didn't know what to say as the session ended.

A few weeks later, Rene asked if he could meet with the business owner. When they met, the employee started by saying, "I finally found my brother's killer." The owner's heart sank, expecting to hear that Rene had taken the man's life. The employee said that he had indeed made preparations to exact revenge, but that the discussion about forgiveness had haunted him. And when the moment finally came, his heart wouldn't let him go through with it. Instead, Rene chose to forgive the man. Not only did it save another life, but it also finally began the healing process for the one who forgave him, and it changed the lives of everyone in two families by breaking the cycle of violent revenge.

GOOD VALUES ALWAYS VALUE PEOPLE

How do you know whether a value is good? There's one standard that it must meet. It must value people—all people, all of the time, in all situations. No shortcuts, no rationalizations, no exceptions. If the value values people, then it is positive and worth embracing. If it devalues people in any way, it's not a good value. Good values always align with the golden rule. As Millard Fuller, founder of Habitat for Humanity, said, "For a community to be whole and healthy, it must be based on people's love and concern for each other."[14] Good values are the foundation of that community. They are inclusive, not excluding anyone. They draw people together despite differences in race, ethnicity, religion, or political views.

Unfortunately, many people in our world feel devalued instead of valued by others, and it harms them deeply. It keeps them from enjoying life and reaching their potential. That was the case for Cristian Molina, an eighteen-year-old living in Costa Rica. When he was a boy, he was often bullied. He changed schools, but it didn't help.

Things were just as bad at home. His father and stepmother mistreated him. His treatment was no better with his mother. They constantly told him he was no good, stupid, useless, and a failure. His father forced him to drop out of school to work when he was sixteen. He tried to go to school at night to try to better his life, but his father repeatedly told him that he was wasting his time trying to learn. Finally, one day his father came to the shop where he worked, and in front of all his coworkers, his father said, "You're not only going to fail your school test, but you're going to end up on the street, looking for work that will only just barely keep you alive. Don't ever think about having children because you won't be able to give them a decent life."

That prompted Cristian to make a decision. He had been learning values, and he remembered what he had learned about having a positive attitude. "Having a positive attitude is essential," said Cristian. "Not only does it determine your level of satisfaction as a person, but it also has an impact on the way others interact with you." Cristian moved out of his father's house and instead lived with his aunt. He was determined not to allow others to abuse him. He was inspired by another lesson he'd learned at the table. "You can make your life a great story," he said. He is doing exactly that, and because of the values he's learned, he has a better understanding of his own value. "Now I like to help friends with advice and my experiences. There are people who have made better decisions and have improved their quality of life thanks to my story."

> WE ARE PEOPLE OF VALUE WHO VALUE OTHERS AND ADD VALUE TO THEM.

There are few things in life more important than valuing people. In fact, this standard of valuing people is the cornerstone of my organizations. I stress it to my staff. I insist on it in my leaders. When I train new members of the John Maxwell Team to become certified as coaches and speakers, I emphasize it. I tell them, "We are people of value who value others and add value to them. Everything we do must live up to this standard."

GOOD VALUES MUST BE PERSONAL

In his book *Awaken the Leader Within*, Bill Perkins described the differences between practices, principles, and values:

> A practice is an activity or action that may work in one situation but not necessarily in another. Unlike a practice, a value applies to every situation.
>
> Values are also different from principles. A principle is an *external* truth that is as reliable as a physical law such as the law of gravity. When Solomon said, "A gentle answer turns away wrath, but a harsh word stirs up anger," he stated a principle that is both universal and timeless. . . .
>
> While we may acknowledge the reliability of many principles, we only internalize those we deem important. When that happens, the principle has become a value that serves as the *internal* map we use to direct our lives. A value, then, is an internalized principle that guides our decision.[15]

My friend Dianna Kokoszka, who for years has been a coach and mentor to some of the best real estate brokers and agents at Keller Williams, recently told me about something she did after hearing me speak about values. She wanted to do a bit of self-evaluation to determine where she was living up to her values and where she wasn't. "I went home and wrote down my values, wrote the definition I have for that value, and then went through each, writing where I had demonstrated this value well, and evaluating where I had not demonstrated them to the fullest," said Diana. "This exercise helped me focus on what mattered most in my life." She put those values where she could see them every day to remind herself of what she stood for and to reinforce her actions. "Taking a stand for others is very important to me, and I will believe in people's potential greatness more than they will believe in their limitations. I do that by focusing on my values."

> "A VALUE, THEN, IS AN INTERNALIZED PRINCIPLE THAT GUIDES OUR DECISION."
> —BILL PERKINS

If you want to change your world, you must internalize good values yourself before you will be able to change anything outside of you. As Rob says, transformed people transform communities. Positive transformation comes from living out what never changes in a time when everything around you seems to be changing.

GOOD VALUES CREATE STABILITY

There's an old saying: an empty bag doesn't stand up straight. Without values, a person is empty and weak. A lot of people hope that jobs, education, technology, and financial advantages will create the strength to hold up the "bag" of our culture. But you can't depend on these things. For example, if you look at the city of Palo Alto in Silicon Valley, you might expect it to be a paradise. After all, it is the crucible for new technology. It hosts the headquarters of companies like Tesla, Hewlett-Packard, and Houzz. The city's population is highly educated, unemployment is low, and average salaries are high. Sadly, so is the suicide rate. Teen suicides occur in Palo Alto at four times the national average. And they have been known to occur in clusters. Experts continue to search for solutions to the problem.[16]

Good values provide structure and meaning. They also help people to live more stable lives. The Organization for Economic Cooperation and Development (OECD) recognized this.

Historically, OECD has focused on poverty reduction and economic development. But it has recently changed its focus to include a new learning framework, which includes the teaching of values such as responsibility, self-control, empathy, cooperation, and self-efficacy.[17] Why did they make a shift to include values? Because without good values, their work cannot be sustained.

> TRANSFORMED PEOPLE TRANSFORM COMMUNITIES. POSITIVE TRANSFORMATION COMES FROM LIVING OUT WHAT NEVER CHANGES IN A TIME WHEN EVERYTHING AROUND YOU SEEMS TO BE CHANGING.

Values not only help people to live better, they also help people to stay true to themselves. Life is a marathon, not a sprint. You have to be able to sustain yourself, to keep yourself going, to continue pursuing your vision. Now that I am in my seventies, people ask me, "Why do you continue to work so hard to lead and encourage others to live significant lives?" My answer is that my values strengthen me and keep my vision going.

In his book *First Things First*, Stephen R. Covey wrote, "There is no shortcut. But there is a path. The path is based on principles revered throughout history. If there is one message to glean from this wisdom, it is that a meaningful life is not a matter of speed or efficiency. It's much more a matter of what you do and why you do it, than how fast you get it done."[18] What you do, why you do it, and how you do it are based on your values. If your values are good, your life will be stable.

Good values have to become part of a culture for it to be lasting. We like how author Diane Kalen-Sukra described the way values and culture interact. She observed, "Culture . . . is like a forest. The seeds are your core values. Once they take root as behaviours, they can grow into trees, populating your cultural forest. Bad seeds produce unhealthy forests, infertile, and plagued by infestations. Good seeds produce a healthy forest and ecosystems that support life. One is sustainable, the other is simply not."[19]

Something that happened in March 2020 in Birmingham, Alabama, is a testament to good values and how they create a positive culture in an organization. In this case, the organization is Church of the Highlands, led by my friend Chris Hodges, who has created a culture of caring that has made Highlands known across the state as a church that "gets stuff done."[20] It's especially well known in Birmingham for its Dream Center, which helps thousands of people by providing home repairs, food delivery, tutoring, job training, and other services. I've been connected to churches my entire life, yet I've never seen anything like Highlands. When members of Highlands see needs in their community, they are continually encouraged by Chris and his staff to do something about it—to provide leadership, start a program, and recruit volunteers. It's incredible.

So it was not surprising what happened during the rise of the COVID-19 pandemic. Robert Record, a medical doctor who works for Highlands and is the CEO of a health clinic that the church helped create, was seeing patients who had coronavirus symptoms, but he had no way to test them. He wanted to do something about that, and he knew that local health care systems in Birmingham would not be able to provide testing on the scale that would be needed.

Record contacted his friend Ty Thomas of Assurance Scientific Laboratories, also a Highlands member, and together they talked to Chris Hodges about doing something. They quickly formed a plan for providing COVID-19 testing. Less than forty-eight hours later, with the help of ten workers from the clinic, three testing lab workers, twenty church staff members, and more than a hundred volunteers, the operation was up and running in one of the church's parking lots.

People flocked to the location to be tested. "One of our goals is that people not go into a doctor's office and not go into a hospital if they don't have to," said Record.[21] Highlands set up shortwave radio so that drivers could tune to an FM station for instructions. They were told to remain in their cars with the windows rolled up until they had been carefully screened. Doctors spoke with patients using cell phones and evaluated them through their car windows. On the first day, they sent two people in respiratory distress to the hospital, one of whom was put on a ventilator.

Their parking lot testing center remained open for four days. In that time, they tested two thousand people, far more than the capacity of any hospital or health facility in the region at the time. Who knows how many lives they saved?

One of Highlands's values is helping people however they can. "We're committed to serving the needs of our community," said Chris. "We were blessed to have leaders trained, financial margin, along with facility space and dozens of staff and volunteers willing to serve." Based on social media posts and the many handmade thank-you signs pressed against car windshields, the community was grateful.

This kind of activity by Highlands is typical; it simply shows their values in action and illustrates the power of what happens when transformed people work together to make a difference. It shows that good values are universal and that the stability they provide creates a strong foundation people can use to change their world.

Good Values Establish Trust

For many years Rob has been very successful in developing life-giving programs through OneHope. One of the reasons for that comes from his ability to build positive relationships. He and I were talking about that, and here is what he shared with me:

> For partnerships to thrive, trust must be the foundation. Movements move at the speed of trust because they are dependent upon the collaboration process.
>
> I see the trust in these kinds of positive relationships as being a three-legged stool relying on the values of generosity, humility, and integrity. To work together, we must have all three.
>
> - Generosity: giving up resources for the whole.
> - Humility: giving up your own importance, position, and power.
> - Integrity: truthfulness so that others can depend on your character.
>
> I really believe these are the characteristics that form the bedrock of who we work with, where we work together, and how we get things done.

Rob and I are on the same page about the importance of trust. As we talked, he reminded me of something that happened as we were working to expand our transformation program through the JMLF. Leaders from one country asked us to come and lead transformation tables there, so we went through our vetting process. After our initial visit, we decided not to partner with them. Why? Because they lacked those three values.

We did not feel that we could establish a trusting partnership with them.

I've learned a lot over the years from reading the book of Proverbs because it contains so much practical wisdom. Its pages are filled with insight into values, including the three Rob shared:

> **Generosity** is the *fuel* for transformation. It is the opposite of selfishness. Proverbs says, "A generous person will prosper; whoever refreshes others will be refreshed."
>
> **Humility** is the *spirit* of transformation. It is the opposite of pride. Proverbs says, "When pride comes, then comes disgrace, but with humility comes wisdom."
>
> **Integrity** is the *strength* of transformation. It is the opposite of deceit. Proverbs says, "The integrity of the upright guides them, but the unfaithful are destroyed by their duplicity."

No matter what you want to do—whether it's raising a family, building a business, or changing your world—you need to develop trust. That comes only with good values.

GOOD VALUES ARE BETTER LIVED THAN SPOKEN

A friend shared a copy of a company's values with me and asked me what I thought about them. Here's what it said:

> **Respect**
> We treat others as we would like to be treated ourselves.
> We do not tolerate abusive or disrespectful treatment.
> Ruthlessness, callousness and arrogance don't belong here.
> **Integrity**
> We work with customers and prospects openly,

honestly, and sincerely. When we say we will do something, we will do it; when we say we cannot or will not do something, then we won't do it.

Communication

We have an obligation to communicate. Here, we take the time to talk with one another . . . and to listen. We believe that information is meant to move and that information moves people.

Excellence

We are satisfied with nothing less than the very best in everything we do. We will continue to raise the bar for everyone. The great fun here will be for all of us to discover just how good we can really be.[22]

I thought it was clear, succinct, and powerful. "Wow!" I said. "That sounds like a great company. Who is it?"

"You'll never guess," she answered with a smile. "Enron!"

That was a shocker. Enron's failure in 2001 was catastrophic. At the time, it was the largest corporate bankruptcy and shakeup that had ever occurred in the financial world. Shareholders lost $74 billion. Many of Enron's employees, whose entire retirement funds were invested in Enron stock, were wiped out financially. The organization's corporate officers were convicted of obstruction of justice, conspiracy, securities fraud, bank fraud, wire fraud, and insider trading; they spent years in prison.[23] Their actions stood in stark contrast to their published values.

Here's the reality. *For leadership to be good and lasting, it must be preceded by good living. Good living comes from good values.* If there's a disconnect between what you say is important and what you do, then teaching values is worthless. So is rhetoric. The actions we take are what give us real credibility. That's why we believe the most important words any leader can say are "Follow me." When our words are backed up with consistency in our actions, we gain credibility. As nineteenth-century writer Wallace Wattles said, "The world needs demonstration more than instruction." There is no substitute for making values our own and living them out every day of our lives.

GOOD VALUES CHANGE YOUR WORLD

I want to share a story that represents the opposite of what happened at Enron. It's about Bantrab, a large bank with 157 branches and more than 4,200 employees in Guatemala.[24] In 2014 Juan Pablo de León, the human resources director at Bantrab, began interacting with Guatemala Próspera and the John Maxwell Leadership Foundation. He wanted to bring our roundtable curriculum to the bank to teach values such as responsibility, dependability, honesty, patience, hard work, listening, and forgiveness. In 2014, Bantrab began by training 331 leaders to facilitate values roundtables, which we now call transformation tables. Those leaders then took 2,792 of their employees, whom they call associates, through a process where they learned about good values, discussed them openly, assessed themselves on how well they lived those values, and articulated how they wanted to grow in each of the values they were studying.

The hope was that the emphasis on positive values would help the employees and improve the bank's performance. But the results far exceeded even their wildest expectations. In the first year, Bantrab experienced a 3 percent growth in its net promoter score, an indicator of customer experience and predictor of business growth. Soon the company was ranked in the top three for

ROA (return on assets) and ROE (return on equity) for the financial market in Guatemala. Its financial portfolio has grown 19.82 percent since the values project started. And it has received the Great Place to Work Institute certificate for its third consecutive year. It is currently ranked second in its category for all of Central America and the Caribbean.

The transformation of Bantrab was so impacting that de León decided to incorporate values roundtables into the onboarding process of the company so that everyone would share common values and a common vocabulary. Now more than 4,400 employees, their families, and associate partners have participated in roundtables and learned values.[25] And for the last two years Bantrab has organized events for fifteen hundred business clients, where I've had the privilege of speaking at those events and sharing about how values improve company culture, financial innovation, social impact, and inclusion.

The CEO of Bantrab, Michel Caputi, was so excited about how good values had changed his company that he wanted to share with other business leaders what had happened. He invited fifteen hundred of the banks' business clients to an event and commissioned me to speak to them about values. When he introduced me, he told the audience that three things had resulted at Bantrab because of the values transformation tables. First, it has experienced its best year financially because people were living the values they had learned. Second, the company had developed a leadership culture. Previously there had always been a deficit of leaders in the organization, but because people took turns facilitating the values roundtables, leaders were emerging and taking on greater roles. Third, the families of their employees were transforming. Because their employees were sharing the values with their spouses, children, and parents, families were changing before their eyes.

GOOD VALUES MAKE YOU MORE VALUABLE

If you were looking for a friend, would the person's values be important to you? How about a life partner? What about if you needed to hire someone: would their values be important? If you were moving into a new neighborhood, would the values of the people living there be important to you? Of course they would be. Can you think of any situation where good values would *not* be an asset?

Good values always add value to us. And they make us more valuable to others. You can work with someone whose skills are weak if their values are good. You can train someone who is inexperienced as long as they value growth. You can trust someone who makes mistakes if the person is honest. But when good values are absent in someone, working with them becomes very difficult.

Management consultant Richard Barrett said, "Organisational transformation begins with the personal transformation of the leaders. Organisations don't transform; people do!"[26] Communities change the same way—person by person—with the leaders changing first and then inviting others to change with them.

Rob and I have been privileged with front-row seats to observe changes in several communities. That has come about as the result of our organizations OneHope, EQUIP, and the JMLF. OneHope has worked with children and youth teaching them good values for many years. EQUIP has focused on training leaders. The JMLF has launched transformation tables in many countries. So when Rob approached me several years ago to discuss working together to create a leadership values curriculum for youth, I loved the idea. Since everything rises and falls on leadership, I believe if you teach young people to become better leaders, they can add value to others and improve their communities. Our teams worked together and created Lead Today, where teens would learn about influence, vision, integrity, growth, initiative, self-discipline, timing, teamwork, attitude, priorities, relationships, responsibility, communication, and developing leaders.

Rob suggested we pilot Lead Today in Ghana, one of the most influential nations in western Africa. From there he wanted to expand it to other parts of Africa and then beyond. But one of the challenges we faced was the reluctance of young people to become leaders. As Rob said, "When Ghana's teens contemplated leadership, they thought of position, abuse of power, bribery, and corruption." In fact, according to the research OneHope conducted in much of Africa, students considered the ability to influence the lives of other people to be one of the *least important* values for their future. Additionally, in Ghanan culture it was generally believed that young people were expected to take a back seat to older adults when it came to leading others and changing their community. One of the reasons we called the program Lead Today was that we wanted young people to know that it's never too soon to use your influence to create positive change.

> "ORGANISATIONS DON'T TRANSFORM; PEOPLE DO!"
> —RICHARD BARRETT

In 2016 the program was tested in six sites across Ghana with 173 students from the ages of twelve to twenty-one. By the time the students finished learning the leadership values, OneHope recorded the following results:

- In nineteen of twenty-four character strengths measured, average scores of the students rose significantly.
- 86 percent of the participants now considered themselves to be effective leaders, an increase of more than 11 percent.
- Participants showed a significant 90 percent knowledge gain from the leadership training.

- 92 percent of the participants reported they had experienced growth as leaders.[27]
- 100 percent of the participants now considered themselves to be leaders.[28]

With the success of Lead Today measured and validated, OneHope began rolling out the curriculum throughout Ghana and then in other countries. As of 2019 the leadership values curriculum had reached 3.6 million young people in sixty-one countries on six continents in seventeen languages.

More important, we are seeing members of the community changed as a result of learning and living good values. One of my favorite stories Rob has shared is that of Eric, an orphan in Kenya. Eric and his older brothers constituted what's known as a child-led household, because they had no parents and they had to struggle on their own to survive. They all worked on a village farm just to have something to eat. Eric attended school, but he was an outcast, rejected by the other children because of his extreme poverty.

But Eric was fortunate to participate in the Lead Today program at his high school. There he discovered he could become a leader. Today Eric is the elected chairman of a local student charity that helps children in need by providing school fees and supplies.

"Lead Today totally changed my life," said Eric. "Before, it seemed my life was full of challenges. Now I am living a life anyone would like to live!" In the future, he wants to become a civil engineer so he can earn enough money to launch a school and rehabilitation home for orphans.

There is no more important mission than giving others the chance to dream of a better life and equip them to live it. There is no better way to do that than to help them identify, embrace, and live good values. The longer I live, the more I travel the world, the more I work to add value to people, the more I realize how important it is to help others understand the value of good values. I think I used to take values for granted. I grew up in a home with good values, with ethical, hardworking parents who loved me unconditionally and taught me the golden rule. But now I never take values for granted. It's why I've dedicated myself to teaching them. So has Rob. We've found that when you live good values,

Your mind will think things that will help you create positive change.

Your eyes will see things that will help you create positive change.

Your heart will feel things that will help you create positive change.

Your attitude will embrace things that will help you create positive change.

Your mouth will say things that will help you create positive change.

Your life will attract things that will help you create positive change.

Your feet will lead you to do things that will create positive change.

If you haven't had the benefit of being raised in a home with good values, like Rob and I were, know that we believe you can and will learn and embrace good values. We've found that the best place for that to happen is at transformation tables, which we'll tell you about in the next chapter. As soon as you're living and modeling good values, you'll be able to help others to do the same. That, more than anything else, will bring the lasting change you want to see in your world.

CHAPTER 6

TRANSFORMATION HAPPENS ONE TABLE AT A TIME

The table is a place where everyone helps everyone improve.

Because we've always wanted to make a difference, Rob and I have worked to help people for most of our lives. Through the years, I've approached that goal in many different ways. I've counseled people one-on-one. I've taught. I've created staff training programs. I've hosted conferences and seminars. I've spoken at large events. I've built organizations. I've written books. I've created resources on paper, audiotape, videotape, DVD, and internet platforms. After more than fifty years, I've come to a conclusion: transformation happens one table at a time.

Now, don't get me wrong, this isn't my last book. And I'm not done speaking or creating resources. All those things have value—and have the power to add value to people—so I'll keep doing them. But the most dramatic, penetrating, and long-lasting changes I've ever seen have come around a table with a small group of people.

LIFE IS BETTER AT THE TABLE

Maybe I should have figured this out sooner. I know that the good values my brother, sister, and I learned from my parents were formed around the dinner table, where we talked every night. Many of the lessons that formed my thinking and my leadership were learned around a small conference table in a circle of leaders. And some of the best mentoring sessions I've led have been with a few people around a table where we were honest and vulnerable, speaking freely and learning from one another. It's also said that the fastest way to find common ground with an enemy is to sit at the table and break bread with them. Change happens around the table.

For the last nine years, my nonprofit organizations have used this awareness to change the way they do things. They have made values-based training the centerpiece of community transformation by gathering small groups of people around a table—or in a small circle—to discuss and share the values they are learning and putting into practice. We have come to call these small groups transformation tables. So far 1.3 million people have sat around 200,000 of these tables, and the positive changes we have seen are amazing.

As I've said, we started this process in Guatemala. At Patsy, a forty-year-old restaurant chain famous for their whipped cream cakes with strawberries, the owners of the company wanted to invest in their staff of more than six hundred workers at twenty-three locations. They created a personal growth resource library for their employees, and in 2016 Patsy started hosting transformation tables with the JMLF curriculum.

Teamwork and productivity surged. Monthly usage of library materials went up 400 percent in one year. One in ten of their workers decided to continue their education. And 99 percent of their staff credited the values they learned at their transformation tables with increasing personal and professional satisfaction in their lives. What Facebook COO Sheryl Sandberg said is true: "Talking can transform minds, which can transform behaviors, which can transform institutions."[1]

COME TO THE TABLE

If you want to help people to transform their lives, then you will want to learn how to gather small groups around a table and get them talking about good values and how to apply them to their everyday lives. Here's how transformation tables work and how you can start using them to change your world.

1. TRANSFORMATION TABLES START SMALL

Big things come from small beginnings. A movement can begin with a single person: you. One of the fantastic things about transformation tables is that anyone, anywhere can start using them to create transformation. You don't need an organization or an education or even formal training. You don't need to launch a bunch of groups. You just need to be able to answer two questions. Do you think your community will improve if you improve yourself? Do you think others want to improve their lives?

> BIG THINGS COME FROM SMALL BEGINNINGS.

If you answer yes to those two questions, you're ready to start, and you can begin with as few as four people. Just invite three others to the table, commit to growing together, identify what you want to learn, and get started. (If you want to lead a round-table using the free curriculum the John Maxwell Leadership Foundation has developed, then go to ChangeYourWorld.com and let us know you're interested in becoming a facilitator.)

2. TRANSFORMATION TABLES PROVIDE COMMON GROUND FOR PEOPLE

Everything good in human interaction starts with common ground. It's where connections are made, relationships are built, trust is formed around shared values, and progress begins. Transformation tables provide the fertile soil where growth happens because they offer a place and time for people to gather for a common purpose.

Someone who values the power of common ground is Tina L. Singleton, the founder and executive director of a nonprofit organization called Transformation Table. Her mission is to use food as a way to bridge differences and facilitate genuine human connection.

Tina has lived her life connecting with people, serving them, and including people who are often marginalized. For many years she served in the Peace Corps as a community development volunteer, and early on she discovered that she wanted to work with people who had disabilities when she connected with a deaf man in a market in Benin. She discovered her passion for working with people who have disabilities. Over the course of her career, she has helped and provided support to people in the Central African Republic, Benin, the Republic of Congo, Bangladesh, Libya, Sierra Leone, Costa Rica, Togo, and Afghanistan.

It was in Afghanistan she really understood the power of finding common ground by sitting around a table together for a meal. While working in that country, she grew a garden. Inexperienced gardener that she was, she grew far too much produce for her own use, so she started giving some away, then hosting lunches. In war-zone countries like Afghanistan, foreigners working for NGOs are often housed in security compounds that isolate them from local citizens. Tina crossed those barriers by eating in Afghani homes and inviting both locals and expats to dine with her. She witnessed connections made, barriers removed, and deeper relationships developed.

But it wasn't until a few years later, after she had moved to Charleston, South Carolina, that she got the idea for starting Transformation Table to bring together diverse people for a meal. Tina heard Bernice King speak at an event commemorating the 2015 massacre at the city's Mother Emanuel AME Church. King said that if the diverse groups in Charleston were serious about loving and understanding one another, they needed to be more intentional and meet more often or have dinner together. Recalling her experience in Afghanistan, Tina found herself thinking, *I wonder if I can do something like that here.*

In November 2016 Tina hosted her first transformation table dinner in a friend's home. It comprised a diverse group, and their meal was prepared by a Vietnamese chef. She hosted another meal the next month with ten strangers and a different chef. Then another. She is still doing them. Every month she brings together a group of ten strangers to eat a meal prepared by a chef in someone's home. Her desire is to see people live in unity who might otherwise be divided, so she gives them an opportunity to develop acceptance, rapport, compassion, peace, and trust by sharing a meal in a foreign cuisine. She is building bridges in Charleston, but her vision is to see people dining together at her kind of transformation tables in every country around the world so they can find common ground. What a great dream!

This is Tina's way of changing her world. She wants to create a world where everyone feels seen, heard, and understood in a community based on love, compassion, and empathy. Rob and I applaud her. When we started to research her organization, we discovered she had trademarked the term *transformation table*. We were unaware of that, so we immediately reached out to her to request permission to continue to use the term transformation tables for our kinds of tables, and she graciously agreed. We're excited about that because our *transformation tables* are places where people come together to learn values and improve their lives.

The potential for connection is great when people come together at these tables. Here are several of the benefits of being at the table together.

Proximity

You may be able to impress people from a distance, but you can impact them only from up close. Transformation is personal. It requires the investment of one person into another. The most effective facilitators of transformation tables are open, authentic, and vulnerable. They admit their shortcomings and are honest about their failures. They share how they want to grow and change to become a better person who lives better values.

> YOU MAY BE ABLE TO IMPRESS PEOPLE FROM A DISTANCE, BUT YOU CAN IMPACT THEM ONLY FROM UP CLOSE.

There is also an accountability aspect at transformation tables. Each time people meet, they identify how they desire to grow and what they intend to do to follow through. The next time they meet, they ask one another how they did. The ideal table is the type where people are physically together in one place. However, because of technology, it's possible to have a "table" with people connecting from different locations.

Environment

Motivation is overrated; environment matters more. We become like the people we spend our time with. If you grew up in a family of intellectuals, you probably tend to be a thinker who likes ideas. If you spend all your time around fit athletes, you probably value fitness and work to stay in shape. If your social circle is filled with high-caliber businesspeople, you probably talk about business and have a knack for it. If you're an artist, you probably gravitate toward other artists, and it fuels your creativity.

At transformation tables where a facilitator leads a discussion on values, people examine their past behaviors and become more self-aware by talking about good values and how to apply them to their lives. This environment encourages growth and change because people get to see what other people do. As professors Nicholas A. Christakis and James H. Fowler stated in their book *Connected*, "Our interconnection is not only a natural and necessary part of our lives but also a force for good. Just as brains can do things that no single neuron can do, so can social networks do things that no single person can do."[2]

Repetition

Change is never instantaneous. It takes time and it takes repetition. James Clear has written a fantastic book titled *Atomic Habits*, which I strongly recommend. In it he wrote about how habits are formed:

Each time you repeat an action, you are activating a particular neural circuit associated with that habit. This means that simply putting in your reps is one of the most critical steps you can take to encoding a new habit. . . .

All habits follow a similar trajectory from effortful practice to automatic behavior, a process known as *automaticity*. Automaticity is the ability to perform a behavior without thinking about each step, which occurs when the nonconscious mind takes over.

It looks something like this:

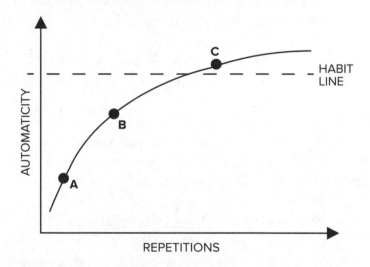

Clear notes that with enough practice an activity passes the habit line when the behavior is done without requiring thinking. He goes on to say the learning curves reveal that habits are based on frequency, not time. He wrote,

One of the most common questions I hear is, "How long does it take to build a new habit?" But what people really should be asking is, "How *many* does it take to form a new habit?" That is, how many repetitions are required to make a habit automatic?

There is nothing magical about time passing with regard to habit formation. It doesn't matter if it's been twenty-one days or thirty days or three hundred days. What matters is the rate at which you perform the behavior. You could do something twice in thirty days, or two hundred times. It's the frequency that makes the difference. . . . You need to string together enough successful attempts until the behavior is firmly embedded in your mind and you cross the habit line.

In practice, it doesn't really matter how long it takes for a habit to become automatic. What matters is that you take the actions you need to take to make progress.[3]

Transformation tables provide a common place for participants to get in their repetitions. By meeting regularly, discussing and embracing values, and *taking the actions* needed to make progress, everyone at the table engages in the process of change.

3. TRANSFORMATION TABLES RE-FORM AND REINFORCE PEOPLE'S IDENTITIES

Values are at the core of every person's identity. Because transformation tables focus on good values, they reinforce the positive aspects of a participant's identity. But they also help people to re-form their identities, when good values replace poor ones.

> LEARNING CURVES REVEAL THAT HABITS ARE BASED ON FREQUENCY, NOT TIME.

In Atomic Habits, Clear also wrote about

how a person's identity is formed, which we find very insightful. He observed,

> Your identity emerges out of your habits. You are not born with preset beliefs. Every belief, including those about yourself, is learned and conditioned through experience.
>
> More precisely, your habits are how you embody your identity. . . . The more you repeat a behavior, the more you reinforce the identity associated with that behavior. In fact, the word identity was originally derived from the Latin words *essentitas*, which means *being*, and *identidem,* which means *repeatedly.* Your identity is literally your "repeated beingness."[4]

Clear goes on to write about how the best way of achieving change is to do it from the inside out, whereas most people attempt it from the outside in. They emphasize outcomes, which are external, or they focus on processes, which are the next layer deep. Instead, they should focus on changing identity first. Clear observed,

> Outcomes are about what you get. Processes are about what you do. Identity is about what you believe. When it comes to building habits that last . . . the problem is the *direction* of change.
>
> Many people begin the process of changing their habits by focusing on *what* they want to achieve. This leads us to outcome-based habits. The alternative is to build identity-based habits. With this approach, we start by focusing on *who* we wish to become . . .
>
> On any given day, you may struggle with your habits because you're too busy or too tired or too overwhelmed or hundreds of other reasons. Over the long run, however, the real

reason you fail to stick with habits is that your self-image gets in the way. This is why you can't get too attached to one version of your identity. Progress requires unlearning. Becoming the best version of yourself requires you to continuously edit your beliefs, and to upgrade and expand your identity.[5]

As Clear pointed out, nobody's identity is set in stone. We all have the power to change our beliefs about ourselves, which means we all have the power to change our lives.

Charlie Wetzel, who has helped me write books for more than twenty-five years, shared an insight with me about this concept of changing your core identity by changing the way you think about yourself. He explained how important it was to him when he decided to quit smoking.

> NOBODY'S IDENTITY IS SET IN STONE. WE ALL HAVE THE POWER TO CHANGE OUR BELIEFS ABOUT OURSELVES, WHICH MEANS WE ALL HAVE THE POWER TO CHANGE OUR LIVES.

He had started smoking cigarettes in junior high school at age thirteen or fourteen, and by his late twenties, he was a two-and-a-half-pack-a-day smoker. More than once he tried to quit. He'd give up smoking for a few weeks, but he'd break down and buy a pack and be right back at it again. He said what finally helped him get over the hump was the day he threw away his cigarettes for the last time and told himself, "I'm a nonsmoker, not a smoker who's trying to quit."

Charlie said that quitting was one of the most difficult things he's ever done, but one of the most important. That thought—*I'm a nonsmoker*—is what carried him through. It's been more than thirty years since he quit, and he has advised many people who've said they wanted to quit to change their thinking about themselves by re-forming their identities as nonsmokers.

That's why transformation tables work—because they help people to change how they think about themselves. When people meet regularly at transformation tables to examine, discuss, and apply good values to their lives every week, they are changing their perspective about their identities. They are creating a core of good values within themselves and beliefs about themselves that impact every aspect of their lives. But it starts with making the choice to change.

A few years ago, JMLF launched a three-year values-based program called iLead for youth in Guatemala. Nearly half a million middle school students are currently participating in iLead round-tables. In 2018 we launched it in Paraguay with thirty thousand students. That doubled the next year. The curriculum for the first year is called iChoose, and it's about choosing good values. That's no accident. We started with that framework because we wanted the students to know that growing and improving is an active choice every person has to make if they want to improve their lives and the lives of others around them. The same is true for us.

4. TRANSFORMATION TABLES CONNECT AWARENESS TO APPLICATION FOR PEOPLE

When people come to transformation tables, one of the most important aspects of the process is how they are prompted to create a connection between self-awareness and application. Dawn Yoder with Global Priority Solutions, whom I mentioned in chapter 4, developed the Round Table Methodology™ process we use to help participants do this.

First, participants learn about a good value—what it is, how it can benefit them, how it can positively impact others, and how it can improve their world. But the process doesn't stop there. All the people in the group are asked to examine themselves in light of what they have learned. This is where the process of change really begins. They take a good look at themselves and are asked to evaluate themselves on a scale of one to five. And they're asked to share that self-assessment with the other members of the group.

This is key. Everyone is asked to contribute at the table. Why? If you've ever tried to lead a team or work with a group where one of the team members refused to talk or engage, then you know how frustrating that can be. Disengaged people rarely grow or stimulate growth in others around them. But when people are open and engaged, incredible things happen. Each person's contribution provides perspective to the others in the group. The result? Everyone's awareness about themselves increases.

Once all the people in the group, including the facilitator, have shared where they need to grow, everyone is asked to state what action they need to take to begin changing and growing in that area and how they will specifically follow through with it in the coming week. And the next time everyone comes together at the table, they ask one another to share whether they followed through. In this way, everyone holds one another accountable. It is through these intentional actions that change becomes permanent. Repeated application by each person compounds their improvement.

Rob has pointed out that all recovery groups are built on this concept, many of which, such as Alcoholics Anonymous and Celebrate Recovery, lead to stunning life transformations. The scientific literature supports the value of these kinds of transformation tables because the shift from awareness to application in a supportive environment of accountability is able to challenge and improve even the most destructive life situations in which people find themselves.

5. TRANSFORMATION TABLES GIVE PEOPLE A WAY TO TRACK TRANSFORMATION

When I was in my late twenties, I heard radio personality Earl Nightingale say, "If you will spend one hour a day every day for five years on the same subject, you will become an expert in that area." Those words fired my imagination. They also changed the trajectory of my life. I knew instantly that I would dedicate myself to studying leadership, because I had seen the impact it could make on other people's lives.

I dove into the subject and spent more than an hour a day on it. I read every book I could get my hands on. I listened to leadership messages to glean everything I could from them. I attended conferences and events where I could hear leaders speak. I started asking leaders in my field if they would meet with me for an hour so I could ask them questions. I did whatever I could to learn about leadership.

When I started this process, the promise that I would become a leadership expert in five years is what pushed me. Because I like to keep goals in front of me to keep me motivated, I thought about that end goal just about every day as I picked up a book or listened to a tape. (Yes, that was in the days of cassette tapes—long before CDs or podcasts.) I was both patient and impatient at those times. I wanted to reach the finish line, but I also knew the only way to get there was to stay engaged in the process.

About halfway through that five-year period, I started to notice something happening. I could tell that my leadership was improving. I was becoming better at strategy. I was gaining confidence in my vision. I was articulating it more clearly. I was becoming better at recruiting leaders. And the teams I was leading were more cohesive, focused, and productive. In short, my growth was compounding, so I was seeing the fruit of the consistent leadership development I was pursuing.

And that's when I experienced another shift in my thinking. I started enjoying my personal growth as a leader. I stopped looking at the calendar and counting down the weeks and months until I hit the five-year mark. Instead of asking, "How much longer will this take?" I started asking myself, "How much farther can I go?" I was no longer focused on reaching a destination. I was focused on developing my potential—an ongoing journey with no end in sight. Years later, when I wrote *The 21 Irrefutable Laws of Leadership*, that lesson learned became the Law of Process: leaders develop daily, not in a day.

Transformation tables give people a similar development path to run on. When you decide you're going to learn to live a certain set of good values, and you commit to doing it with the same group of people every week, you know where you're going, you can see how far you've gone, and based on the results in your life, you can track your progress.

IN THE MORNING, BENJAMIN FRANKLIN ASKED HIMSELF, "WHAT GOOD WILL I DO TODAY?" WHEN HE WENT TO BED, HE ASKED HIMSELF, "WHAT GOOD DID I DO TODAY?"

What values should you focus on? You can adopt the list the JMLF uses to track your progress that we shared in chapter 5. You can focus on a list I used for many years that I called my daily dozen and which I shared in my book *Today Matters*. I got the idea for it from Benjamin Franklin. He used to get up every morning and ask himself, "What good will I do today?" When he went to bed, he asked himself, "What good did I do today?" He judged that good came from a set of personal virtues. To hold himself accountable, he carried a "score sheet" with the thirteen virtues he treasured.

Here is my daily dozen, which each morning I ask myself to practice just for that day:

I will choose and display the right attitudes.
I will embrace and practice good values.
I will communicate with and care for my family.
I will know and follow healthy guidelines.
I will determine and act upon important priorities.
I will accept and show responsibility.
I will make and keep proper commitments.
I will initiate and invest in solid relationships.
I will earn and properly manage finances.
I will deepen and live out my faith.
I will desire and experience self-improvement.
I will plan for and model generosity.

As people engage at transformation tables, there are two important things to keep in mind for tracking progress. The first is consistency. When I started my journey learning leadership, the reason I started growing was that I was consistent. I worked at it every day. Did I ever miss a day? Of course. I'm far from perfect. And life is full of surprises. But I made it a priority to grow every day. And whenever I did miss a day, I was determined never to miss two days in a row. I try to think of it the way an athlete would. Football players are proud of their streak of consecutive games played and baseball players are proud of their streak of games with a hit. But when the streak gets broken, they don't quit. They immediately get back to work and start another streak!

The second thing people can do to keep tracking their progress is to ask themselves, "Does this value help me become the person I want to be? Does this behavior work for or against my desired identity?" Values that conflict with a desired identity are not helpful. The values people learn and live must help them grow toward becoming the best individuals they can be. How can they measure that? By how their story changes. That's what Rob and I have consistently seen as a sign of transformation in the lives of people and their communities. Their lives change for the better, and as a result they help others change.

Let me share just one of the thousands of transformations we witnessed in Guatemala. It's the story of Verónica Chávez, who grew up the oldest of twelve in a rural village with parents who had problems with alcoholism. Often the children went without food. Verónica wanted an education and had dreams of becoming a secretary, but when she finished elementary school at age twelve,

> THE VALUES
> PEOPLE LEARN
> AND LIVE MUST
> HELP THEM
> GROW TOWARD
> BECOMING THE
> BEST INDIVIDUALS
> THEY CAN BE.

her parents took her out of school and put her to work, helping to care for the family. When she was fourteen, she was sent to another city nearly a hundred miles away so she could work as a maid.

Verónica worked for two years, and even though people she respected insisted she would never be anything other than a maid, she moved to Guatemala City. There she continued working as a domestic worker, but she also went back to school to train to become a secretary. After graduating, she started working as a receptionist in a counseling office. That's how she connected with Guatemala Próspera and was invited to become part of one of our transformation tables.

One of the lessons discussed at the table was the value of forgiveness. As she examined her life in light of that value, she realized how wounded she was. She was bitter toward her parents, not only for their drinking and neglect, but also because their actions caused one of her younger brothers to be taken from them. Verónica had needed to fight to keep him from being put in a children's home. Feeling compelled to take action about her lack of forgiveness, she traveled the 175 miles home that weekend to talk to her parents and asked them to forgive her. She also forgave them for the hurts she had suffered. After years of separation, they were united again. And Verónica's wounds began to heal.

Learning the transformation values and living them inspired Verónica to keep dreaming. Her new aspiration was to become a social worker because of what happened with her brother. She enrolled in a university and took courses on the weekend. In 2017 she graduated with a degree in social work.

Verónica is the first woman from her small community to have graduated from a university. She said, "Now, many young men and women from my community see me as a motivation for them to fight for their lives, and they say, 'If she could, then I can too.' I tell everyone that all they need to do is set goals and be consistent because they can do it. Even if people tell you 'You can't do it' or 'you're not capable,' don't listen to them!"

Verónica said, "Learning values at the table has changed not only my life, my family, and my community, but it will change future generations."

When you track your progress, it's easier to see your progress. It's a fact that people who track their progress are more successful than those who don't. People who track their eating lose more weight than those who don't. People who track their workouts progress faster than those who don't. People who track their sales, their production, and their finances perform better than those who don't. And people who track their progress while learning to live good values are more successful both personally and professionally.

6. TRANSFORMATION TABLES HELP PEOPLE DO LIFE BETTER TOGETHER

John D. Rockefeller said, "Don't be afraid to give up the good to go for the great." Learning good values using transformation tables helps people to live better lives. When this happens, the possibility of alleviating poverty, disease, hunger, illiteracy, and other problems within a community increases. Why? Because helping them develop core values that make them happier, healthier, more productive, more content people empowers them to create their own future. They improve their own families and improve their own communities, and that is great!

Any time people get together, whether it's when they form new transformation tables, move to a new neighborhood, accept a new job, or join a new team, they are all internally asking three questions about the people in their lives:

- Do you care for me?
- Can you help me?
- Can I trust you?

People who learn good values at transformation tables become the kind of people who do care, who will help, and who can be trusted. And that creates an environment of encouragement that benefits everyone.

> PEOPLE WHO LEARN GOOD VALUES AT TRANSFORMATION TABLES BECOME THE KIND OF PEOPLE WHO DO CARE, WHO WILL HELP, AND WHO CAN BE TRUSTED.

The table doesn't have to be a literal table. Anyplace where three or more people are willing to get together, get honest, and get to work can be transformational—as long as good values are the foundation for learning and growth. At transformation tables, people who desire to improve their lives gather and

New relationships are formed,

Beliefs are discovered,

Perspective is shared,

Discussions give help,

Questions are asked,

Answers are found,

Trust is given,

Vulnerability is appreciated,

Values are practiced,

Good habits are formed,

Self-worth is increased,

Forgiveness is experienced,

Attitudes are positive,

Responsibility is accepted,

Priorities are identified,

Broken relationships are restored,

Servanthood is lived,
Generosity is shown,
Courage is activated,
Commitments are made,
Initiative is encouraged,
Integrity is valued, and
Lives are changed!

So are you ready to sit at one of our transformation tables? Are you ready to look at yourself, admit where you need to grow, and work on it? Are you willing to invite others to the table so they can join you in this growth journey? If you're ready, step into the process. You can visit our website ChangeYourWorld.com to get the free materials to facilitate transformation at the table. We promise it will change you. And that will change your world.

CHAPTER 7

WHAT GETS DONE GETS MEASURED

Measure what matters.

—JOHN DOERR

Recently I went bowling with some friends. It was so much fun, even though I hadn't bowled in forty years. My friends laughed as they watched me roll the ball in the gutter over and over.

"Maybe we should remove the bowling pins since John's not going to hit them!" one of them taunted.

"No way! I will hit them eventually," I replied. It took a while, but I finally did. I even got a strike, and everyone stood up, cheered, and high-fived me. One even took a photo of the lane with all the pins gone and texted it to me. "Keep the picture so you can remember it," he said. "It may never happen again!"

It was all in good fun, and since I had such a good time, I've often thought about it. And that has prompted me to come to this conclusion: the only reason for bowling a ball down a lane is to see if we can knock down the pins.

For me, the pins make all the difference. As the ball releases from my hand, I watch it to see how well I did. I like that I get the results in mere seconds by counting the pins left standing. If I knock them all down, I celebrate. If I put the ball in the gutter, I'm disappointed. If there are no pins, there is no point.

Maybe you disagree. If you're highly relational, you might be thinking, *The bowling pins are not important. I bowl just for the exercise and social time with my friends.*

But could you really enjoy bowling without pins? Try it. Go out with your friends and keep bowling the ball down the lane at . . . nothing. How long do you think you would keep doing that before you quit? I predict you'd stop pretty quickly. Why? Because the energy and fun of bowling comes from seeing how well you're doing. Without a measurement tool, it isn't worth the effort. There's no joy in it.

WHO'S KEEPING SCORE?

Author and former Gallup researcher Tom Rath recently wrote a book titled *Life's Greatest Question*. It's a kind of sequel to *Now, Discover Your Strengths*, which he coauthored. He was frustrated by the self-focus of many people who used StrengthsFinder to learn about themselves. Many readers made self-satisfaction their focus, whereas Rath believed the purpose of finding your strengths was to add value to people and "make meaningful contributions over a lifetime."[1] In fact, the title of the book was inspired by

> "LIFE'S MOST PERSISTENT AND URGENT QUESTION [IS] *WHAT ARE YOU DOING FOR OTHERS?*"
> —MARTIN LUTHER KING JR.

a speech by Martin Luther King Jr., who said, "Life's most persistent and urgent question [is] 'What are you doing for others?'"[2]

Rath noted, "You can begin by connecting your daily efforts to the way they contribute to specific people's lives—connecting *what you do* with *who your work serves.*" He went on to give examples of how connecting the work we do to the benefits it brings others leads to better results, greater satisfaction, and personal well-being:

> In food service, for example, when a cook or someone preparing food can literally see the people they serve, it increases that customer's satisfaction with the meal by 10%. If the cook and customer can both see one another, satisfaction with meal quality goes up 17% and service is 13% faster. You see a similar result across other professions.
>
> When lifeguards read stories of people's lives being saved, they are more vigilant on the job. When telephone-based fundraisers hear from the beneficiaries of their work, they are more motivated and raise far more funds for their cause. Even when the only people you serve are internal customers or colleagues, connecting the work you do with the direct contribution it makes has tangible benefits.
>
> In a Harvard study, field workers who harvested tomatoes watched videos of the way their contribution helped colleagues in the factory another step down the supply chain. In comparison to a control group, the workers who watched this short video experienced a 7% increase in productivity, as measured by tons of tomatoes harvested per hour. My takeaway from all this research is that people experience a far greater sense of belonging and more sustainable wellbeing when they connect their efforts in the moment with a larger influence on others.[3]

In other words, keeping score matters as much in making a difference as it does in bowling. In all of these examples—bowling pins, cooks, lifeguards, telephone fund-raisers, and tomato pickers—there was one thing in common: keeping score brought energy and fulfillment to people's lives. Measurement matters.

You may have heard the phrase "what gets measured gets managed," which is often attributed to Peter Drucker. It later evolved into "what gets measured gets done," a popular catchphrase in business and manufacturing. For the title of this chapter, we've turned this phrase around. Why? Because in the world of helping people and nonprofit organizations, many people judge their effectiveness based on how their efforts make them feel rather than on results. That's no way to change the world.

> "PEOPLE EXPERIENCE A FAR GREATER SENSE OF BELONGING AND MORE SUSTAINABLE WELLBEING WHEN THEY CONNECT THEIR EFFORTS IN THE MOMENT WITH A LARGER INFLUENCE ON OTHERS."
> —TOM RATH

One of the things I greatly admire about Rob and OneHope is how they *measure* everything they do. At OneHope, what gets done truly gets measured. Rob and his team never assume the work they're doing actually works. No matter how good they feel about what they're *trying* to do, no matter how good their intentions are or how noble their purpose is, they don't assume they're making a difference. They use data to verify what works—and what doesn't.

YOU CAN GOOGLE IT

Investor John Doerr patiently listened as two Stanford grad-school dropouts went through their seventeen-slide deck to pitch him their idea on how to "organize the world's information and make it universally accessible and useful." Doerr immediately forked over $11.8 million in exchange for 12 percent of this revolutionary new idea. That was in 1999.[4] Today, that idea has grown to become the third most valuable company,[5] the second most valuable brand,[6] and the best place to work in the world.[7]

How do you turn a transformational idea into something that can change your world? By measuring it. In the foreword of John Doerr's book *Measure What Matters*, Alphabet CEO and Google cofounder Larry Page—one of those Stanford dropouts—described how Doerr used to help him and his pitching partner, Sergey Brin, turn their slide-deck ideas into the transformation engine that we call Google today. Page said, "As much as I hate process, good ideas with great execution are how you make magic."[8]

This "hated process" is the bedrock for success. That's as true in individual efforts, community involvement, volunteer initiatives, and nonprofit organizations as it is in businesses. The principle of measurement is universal and helps to identify and support the best practices that are at the heart of every successful transformative enterprise.

For Google, measurement came in the form of OKRs (objectives and key results), which were derived from management by objectives (MBO), a goal-setting system developed by Peter Drucker, one of the most widely known influential thinkers on management and systems. John Doerr had learned about them and used them at Intel, he taught them to Larry Page and Sergey Brin, and they transformed the internet—and the world.

MEASURING TRANSFORMATION

It's true that we measure what we treasure. Think about it. Each trip to the doctor includes charting your height and weight, taking your temperature, and checking on your iron or blood sugar. You and your doctor monitor your health because you value it. The same is true for your bank account—you keep an eye on what comes in and goes out, put some away for emergencies, and monitor your investments.

WE MEASURE WHAT WE TREASURE.

If we neglect to measure something we treasure, it won't retain its value. Today Rob's organization is fantastic at measuring everything it does, but it hasn't always been that way. Rob said,

> I didn't realize that I had failed to apply these principles of measurement to our community transformation work until an eye-opening trip to the country that was formerly known as Swaziland, now called the Kingdom of Eswatini. My team and I went to film some of the great work reportedly happening through the character education program that we had developed. The king of the country had given us permission to run the program in every public school, so we

had large numbers of students going through the program. But we didn't realize that the most important numbers were not being measured.

The biggest red flag was the fact that the number of people with HIV/AIDS was rapidly increasing instead of decreasing—to the point that, at that time, the United Nations projected that Swaziland could become the first extinct nation in the entire world if the problem continued to escalate!

I was devastated. With all the organizations—including ours—working in the country to reverse the HIV/AIDS epidemic, it was clear that our activities were not producing the results we had hoped for. After a sleepless night, I came to terms with a harsh realization. While we were working hard, we were hardly making a difference.

Desperate to find answers, I began a journey, a journey I am still on today, to do more than measure activity, but commit myself to measure what matters, to measure results.

Everyone loves to talk about transformation, but the question is this: How do you measure it? The Law of Priorities in *The 21 Irrefutable Laws of Leadership* says leaders understand that activity is not necessarily accomplishment. No matter how you're working to make a difference, measuring results is one of the greatest skills you can develop in becoming a person that can change your world.

> LEADERS UNDERSTAND THAT ACTIVITY IS NOT NECESSARILY ACCOMPLISHMENT.

THE FIVE DS

Rob came away from that experience determined to make everything he and his team did in countries around the world as effective as possible. That meant creating a process of measuring whatever got done. Rob developed a simple framework to ensure that whatever problem he was trying to solve or issue he was addressing or circumstance he was determined to transform, he would gather data, track progress, and measure positive change. It became a process he called the Five *D*s.

> **Discover**—Find out what's really going on and who is doing something about it.
> **Design**—Develop a strategy that begins with the end in mind and builds on your strengths, not your weaknesses.
> **Deploy**—Implement your plan. Start small, fail soon, and adjust often.
> **Document**—Measure to make sure that your intended outcomes are being accomplished.
> **Dream**—Start the cycle over, expanding what works and abandoning what doesn't.

As you can see, the Five-D method is not linear but circular. You don't do it once and stop; rather, it is a process that starts over as soon as you get to the end. You learn to leverage strengths, mitigate weaknesses, and grow both the team and opportunities as you learn and grow through each cycle of improvement.

One of the fantastic things about Rob's method is that it's a system of development that can start small and grow incrementally, transforming as it expands its scope and scale. It's similar to the flywheel effect my friend Jim Collins discussed in his book *Good to Great*. Collins wrote, "No matter how dramatic the end result, good-to-great transformations never happen in one fell swoop. In building a great company or social sector enterprise, there is no single defining action, no grand program, no one killer innovation,

> "NO MATTER HOW DRAMATIC THE END RESULT, GOOD-TO-GREAT TRANSFORMATIONS NEVER HAPPEN IN ONE FELL SWOOP."
> —JIM COLLINS

no solitary lucky break, no miracle moment. Rather, the process resembles relentlessly pushing a giant, heavy flywheel, turn upon turn, building momentum until a point of breakthrough, and beyond."[9]

Let's take a look at each of Rob's *D*s.

1. DISCOVER

Rob says that research is the key that opens the doors to transformational outcomes. But don't let the term *research* put you off. Research is simply a discovery of the truth. It lets you know where you are, what you're dealing with, and how you need to make adjustments. For example, when you discover your bank account is overdrawn, you know you need to stop spending. You pause and take a hard look at your expenses to figure out where to economize, then create a budget that will get you back on track. You stop, look, and listen to what the numbers are telling you.

It's good to slow down and ask the right questions, but not everyone does—or does it well. Some people never want to stop and discover what's true. They just keep moving forward. Others take stock and then jump into action, reacting to a problem without fully understanding it. Others become deer in the headlights—frozen in inaction, not knowing what to do next.

Pausing to discover allows you to take a hard look at what you are doing and figure out what is working, what isn't, and what to do better. During discovery, you're learning how to reach the goal you are trying to achieve. Rob says this pause was a pivotal moment in his personal and professional development because it led him to understand the critical importance of research.

> DURING DISCOVERY, YOU'RE LEARNING HOW TO REACH THE GOAL YOU ARE TRYING TO ACHIEVE.

When we understand the reality of a problem we are trying to solve or how to help the people we are trying to serve, we can begin to chart our next steps. To do this, you don't have to launch a full-scale research initiative. Your *research* might be as quick and easy as doing a few quick searches on the internet to get started. No matter where you start, just be careful not to simply look for numbers and statistics that prove your specific intentions. You have to be open to discovering the truth of your situation, and you have to be willing to pivot your plan to serve the present reality and your cause.

Research Reveals What's Going On

One of the best ways to start some simple research is through discovery conversations. Invest in six cups of coffee to set up six conversations. Talk with an expert. Find someone who's been in the game for a long time. Ask to meet with someone who has been affected by what you're working on. Or spend some time with a unique person who breaks the mold. The secret here isn't the talking part; it's the listening! Listen deeply and ask good follow-up questions. Then look for patterns of what everyone agrees on, especially when the people are from diverse backgrounds and bring unique perspectives.

Research reveals the truth. Rob said,

> I probably say, "research is revelatory" at least five times a day. I say it because I believe it. When you take the time to do your research, you can clearly see the challenges you are facing and communicate them well to your team. Having information in hand creates a shared reality for the team that . . .
> Helps us see the same things.
> Helps us see the same things the same way.
> Helps us see ourselves in a new way.
> Helps us see who else also cares about our cause.
> Helps us see what truly makes a difference.

Too often we make assumptions and keep working. I know I'm sometimes guilty of this. By stopping and doing research in the discovery phase, we're better prepared to make a difference.

Research Helps You to Look at the Hard Truths

Rob says that oftentimes doing research and discovering the truth can be challenging, and in the short term it can even be discouraging. But understanding the truth of the situation we are trying to change, especially one that is dire, requires that we first confront our reality. When we argue with reality, we lose 100 percent of the time.

> WHEN WE ARGUE WITH REALITY, WE LOSE 100 PERCENT OF THE TIME.

It can be difficult for us when we face the hard truth of what we discover. It can be even harder for others. Rob said,

> After doing extensive research prior to launching a new educational program in the nation of Malawi, I presented the country's leaders with a report of our findings. We had found that HIV/AIDS was skyrocketing among children and youth, and there were some shocking shifts in morals. We discovered that many traditional interventions, while created with good intentions, were exacerbating the problem rather than alleviating it.
>
> When we presented our findings, some of the leaders were so angry that they told me I was lying and asked me to leave the meeting. Luckily a great leader and friend of mine, Dr. Lazarus Chakwera, stepped up to the mic, and in the beautiful African tradition asked if he could share a story. He said, "There was a man lost in the African jungle. He wandered for a long time trying to find his way. After many days, he found a little glass mirror on the ground. When he looked into the mirror, he was so disgusted by the dirty, haggard face he saw looking back at him that he threw the mirror on the ground and stomped on it. He hated the reflection the mirror revealed. But my friends and colleagues, the mirror isn't at fault and cannot be blamed for the truth it reveals. The mirror is simply the messenger reflecting the current state of the man."

Research is a mirror, showing us the good, the bad, and the ugly. Rather than getting mad at the mirror, we need to use it as a chance to face the truth. Once we discover the truth, we can take steps to begin effecting change in ourselves, our families, our community, and our world.

Research Helps You to Know Who to Work With

Discovery not only helps us properly assess needs and ask the right questions; it also helps us know who to collaborate with. Rob's organization OneHope launched one of the largest-ever studies of young people in over 150 countries around the world. It was called the Attitudes and Behaviors of Youth (ABY). That study gave them statistical data to reveal the truth of what young people around the world currently thought about many key social issues. This led to the development of a collaborative network. In the midst of surveying and collecting data, they worked with incredible people and organizations from all streams of influence, and many of them became key partners.

Rob and I know that trying to help people make positive changes while going it alone won't work. We need to work with others who are best at what they do while we do what we're best at. Research helps to make this clearer. Rob said,

> This was never clearer to me than when one of the young girls from Swaziland—we'll call her Tinah—broke my heart with a single question after she had begun learning and living good values in one of our programs. She asked, "So what do I do now? Instead of sleeping with the bus driver, should I walk six kilometers to school every day?"
>
> For maybe the first time, Tinah realized that the bus driver was exploiting her sexually, and she keenly felt the injustice of being exploited by men who used their power to abuse her. She knew education would help her, but she was struggling to make the right personal decision, knowing it would threaten her livelihood and that of her family if she stopped going to school. That was a reality if she didn't have a ride there.

It was heartbreaking. My initial response to Tinah's gut-wrenching question was, *I have to start a bus company so these girls can get to school safely.* But while we were doing our research, we discovered an organization called Teen Challenge (now called Challenge Ministries) that was already in place providing safe transportation for students. Instead of starting something that wouldn't be our strength, we partnered with them.

Had we not done our research, we might have duplicated effort and wasted resources by using them to start another bus service when there was already one in existence. Instead, we were able to connect our two programs and multiply our impact in Swaziland.

That's just a single story of how research and collaboration go hand in hand. Rob's and my organizations collaborate everywhere, partnering with organizations and people who are already in place because they are better positioned than we are to understand their context. Sometimes we simply pour resources into them and expand their capacity to help others because that's better stewardship than trying to start from scratch and do it ourselves. Sometimes our research shows there is nothing and no one in place to help fill a need in any given area, so we have to design a new program or process.

As you go through this discovery process, pay attention to who is already working to make a difference in the cause that's calling to you. That's what a mom did when she discovered her son had autism. When she learned that her son was on the spectrum, she felt alone and overwhelmed. So she checked out a stack of books from her local library and started reading all about autism. Then she put some posts out on Facebook to see if anyone else was in the same boat. Within a few days, she had received eleven direct messages of other moms who were feeling just as overwhelmed, lost, and alone on their autism journeys.

Realizing there was a need, she sat down with her husband and made a plan to help resource and encourage the other struggling autism families. They gathered and shared links to local, state, and national groups that were already involved in autism support. She found, joined, and invited the others to online Facebook groups, researched and recommended churches with ministries for people with special needs, and recommended therapists and local support groups. Her efforts have been a great success and help to a lot of families. She didn't need to reinvent the wheel. The main result of her research was sharing it with others.

2. DESIGN

When Bill Gates decided to give the majority of his fortune away, it was to try and fulfill a transformational mission: "Everyone deserves a healthy and productive life."[10] Gates is generous, but he is also very realistic. He has created designs and plans for getting things done his entire life. Gates said, "In philanthropy, I see people confusing *objectives* with *missions* all the time. A mission is directional. An objective has a set of concrete steps that you're intentionally engaged in and actually trying to attain. It's fine to have an ambitious objective, but how do you scale it? How do you measure it?"[11]

One of Rob's favorite shows growing up was *Dragnet*. The star was Detective Joe Friday, played by Jack Webb. When he interviewed witnesses, if they got off track or started giving their opinions, he would say, "Just the facts, ma'am."

Drama and conjecture only muddy the waters when you're trying to get from point A to point B. But when you have the facts

> "I SEE PEOPLE CONFUSING *OBJECTIVES* WITH *MISSIONS* ALL THE TIME. A MISSION IS DIRECTIONAL. AN OBJECTIVE HAS A SET OF CONCRETE STEPS THAT YOU'RE INTENTIONALLY ENGAGED IN AND ACTUALLY TRYING TO ATTAIN."
> —BILL GATES

from your discovery phase, you can quickly cut through the noise and uncertainty of what to do next. Now that you know where you really are, you can work to figure out how to get where you want to go. This clarity provides you with the ability to design solutions grounded in reality. It's a beautiful place to be when you gather information from a range of sources that bring a variety of perspectives and insights to a problem. Once you land on a common consensus for what needs to change and why it needs to change, then you can imagine how it will change. It's helping to create a new story and rewrite the ending.

How do you begin? At the end. "Begin with the end in mind" is one of Stephen R. Covey's seven habits of highly effective people. No matter how much we plan or how hard we work, we'll be truly effective only when we've envisioned what a win looks like in the end. You have to know what your target or destination is before you can get started on the journey.

Yogi Berra famously said, "You've got to be careful if you don't know where you're going, 'cause you might not get there."[12] As funny as this sounds, many people who want to make a difference don't have a process in place or the discipline to get them from where they are now to the transformational ideas they want to act upon. And that's critical. John Doerr put it this way: "Ideas are easy. Execution is everything."

Like anything else in life that we want to see improve, we have to be intentional about it. Success doesn't happen by accident. Thomas Edison said, "I never did anything worth doing by accident, nor did any of my inventions come indirectly through accident, except the phonograph. No, when I have fully decided that a result is worth getting, I go ahead on it and make trial after trial until it comes."[13]

> "IDEAS ARE EASY. EXECUTION IS EVERYTHING."
> —JOHN DOERR

Having been in the business of designing and measuring successful life change programs around the world for nearly three decades, we've broken down the cycle that you start and constantly repeat to ensure your efforts are bringing about the changes you hoped for. Put simply:

1. Describe the reality of where you are, based on the discovery process.
2. Identify your target, where you want to be when you've completed your plan.
3. To the best of your ability, identify all the steps that will be needed to get from your current reality to your target.
4. Identify the people, partners, and resources needed to accomplish those steps.
5. Give yourself an aggressive yet realistic timeline for the completion of your plan with checkpoints along the way.

Without a plan, you won't get specific enough to achieve your goals, and you will end up heading down a thousand wrong trails. Catherine the Great's idealistic children's home is an example of a great idea that went off the rails. Wanting to serve the homeless children of Moscow, the empress commissioned a beautiful building to house street kids. They would be educated, cultivated, and molded into refined and "ideal citizens." However, when many parents saw that their children could have a solid roof over their heads, free meals, clothing, education, and a higher standard of living, they abandoned their children and forced them onto the streets, desiring to give them a better life. Her idea, without careful discovery and design, produced more street kids in Moscow.

You can make a great plan on paper, but like Catherine the Great discovered, it may not work out the way you imagined. How do you guard against that? By building in checkpoints along the way to ensure you're headed in the right direction. And if you discover your plan isn't working out the way you hoped, be prepared to pivot.

3. DEPLOY

There's a danger we need to avoid once we've created a plan for making a difference, and that is this: thinking we're done. We can spend so much time researching and planning that we neglect to get started. Peter Drucker, one of the great analytical designers in the world, warned about this in his book *The Effective Executive*: "One either meets or one works. One cannot do both at the same time."[14]

Once you have created your plan of action, it's time to deploy and see if you can produce the outcomes you desire for changing your world. Deploying is where the action is. The key is to start. Walt Disney didn't waste words when he said, "The way to get started is to quit talking and begin doing."[15]

Begin to implement some of the things you've discovered and designed, but start small. That makes it easier for you to track your progress toward your goal. And if something isn't working, you can change what you're doing and learn as you go.

Rob says that when OneHope was working in Swaziland, tracking their progress along the way was key to making informed choices and positive changes to their program. After a few deployment cycles of

> "ONE EITHER MEETS OR ONE WORKS. ONE CANNOT DO BOTH AT THE SAME TIME."
> —PETER DRUCKER

testing and tweaking a fully redesigned curriculum, they ended up creating a program called I Matter. The program was so successful it was picked up by the government, and the CDC took it and expanded it even beyond what they could. These types of transformational programs are called evidence-based because outcomes are documented.

There's one more thing to keep in mind as you execute your plan. As it does in many other situations, the Pareto principle applies to the results you will see. The Pareto principle says that 20 percent of your priorities will give you 80 percent of your production, *if* you spend your time, energy, money, and personnel on the top 20 percent. So don't expect everything you do to give you an equal return. Most of the change you desire to see will come from only 20 percent of what you're doing.

4. DOCUMENT

Rob and his team really shine when it comes to tracking their progress and documenting the results of what they do. Rob said, "I employ W. Edwards Deming's logic, 'In God I trust; all others must bring data.' In order to figure out what's really going on and how you can make a positive difference, you have to document the results of your activity and ensure they are contributing to the

> "IN GOD I TRUST;
> ALL OTHERS MUST
> BRING DATA."
> —W. EDWARDS DEMING

outcomes you desire. The great thing is that these principles can be applied to any idea, no matter how big or small!"

Because of technology, we are able to measure real-time progress like no other generation in history. People who use a Fitbit know the moment they've hit their exercise goal for the day. Worldometer tracked the spread and recovery from COVID-19 almost in real time. We have access to more and better information than at any other time in human history.

Without properly documenting and tracking your progress, it's impossible to answer these critical questions:

- How many people did our plan impact?
- How did those people change?
- What specific difference did the change make?
- Why did the change occur?

One of the things I've always admired about Rob is his ability to document his work and face the reality of what's working and what's not. When OneHope launched their efforts in Swaziland, their plan looked great on paper. But when he looked at the data that said Swaziland was their most successful program, yet everything in the country was getting worse, he took it as a wake-up call. He didn't try to deny reality or try to justify the work they had done. They documented, dug in, and worked to figure out what was really going on.

It's just as important to document what *doesn't* work. Rob's dad has successfully built more transformative enterprises in his lifetime than we can count. Someone once asked him, "How is it that everything you do prospers?"

His answer? "I have failed more than I have succeeded, and it is on the ashes of those failures that all my success has been built." Rob's father taught him to celebrate his failures even more than his successes. Every time we can pinpoint a misstep, we're that much closer to knowing how to do it better next time. Maya Angelou rightly pointed out: "We may encounter many defeats, but we must not be defeated. It may even be necessary to encounter the defeat, so that we can know who we are."[16]

As you are measuring impact, don't forget to measure areas like ability, credibility, insight, opportunity, and funding. The Susan G. Komen Foundation's solidarity and mobilization can clearly be seen in the pink ribbons on just about everything. So even though they haven't cured breast cancer, they have increased their solidarity and capacity to address the issue more than ever before.

> "I HAVE FAILED MORE THAN I HAVE SUCCEEDED, AND IT IS ON THE ASHES OF THOSE FAILURES THAT ALL MY SUCCESS HAS BEEN BUILT."
> —BOB HOSKINS

As you read about documentation, you may be wondering how anyone goes about measuring transformation. The answer is that big life change comes through a series of small life changes. For the work of the John Maxwell Leadership Foundation, we have the goal of training 1 percent of the population of any country where we work to become roundtable facilitators. We want those facilitators to then train 10 percent of the country's population in good values. That 10 percent is a tipping point.

In his book *The Tipping Point*, Malcolm Gladwell asserts that an idea spreads like a virus after it reaches a certain small percentage. That point, he wrote, "is the moment of critical mass, the threshold, the boiling point."[17] This has been validated scientifically. Scientists at Rensselaer Polytechnic Institute have found that when just 10 percent of the population holds an unshakable belief, their belief will always be adopted by the majority of the society: "When the number of committed opinion holders is below 10 percent, there is no visible progress in the spread of ideas. It would literally take the amount of time comparable to the age of the universe for this size group to reach the majority," said Boleslaw K. Szymanski, the Claire and Roland Schmitt Distinguished Professor at the Department of Computer Science and director of the Social Cognitive Networks Academic Research Center at Rensselaer. "Once that number grows above 10 percent, the idea spreads like flame."[18] The JMLF is currently documenting our efforts in Guatemala, Paraguay, and Costa Rica to measure our progress and validate our work there.

> AN IDEA SPREADS AFTER 10 PERCENT OF PEOPLE ADOPT IT.

Philosopher John Dewey said, "We do not learn from experience . . . we learn from reflecting on experience."[19] As you gather data, document your progress, and analyze what you find, you'll learn about what progress you're making toward your goals.

5. DREAM

When you've documented your progress by gathering information and you've figured out where you're succeeding and where you're failing, you are ready to come full circle. It's time to dream—and to build it bigger and better by rebuilding and refining what you've done. Your progress will give you the momentum to go through the cycle again, but this time with bigger goals in mind.

When Rob and his team get together—he likes to call these meetings dream sessions—they imagine what even more success and impact would look like and how to get there. In these dream sessions, they do the following:

- Add to what they've already learned by digging deeper and learning new information.
- Check to see that they're making progress in the direction they want to go.
- Make sure they're still operating in reality and that things haven't changed so much that they need to change as well.
- Create a roundtable with their core group to help create phase two of the plan, taking what worked and multiplying their efforts in that direction while abandoning what didn't work.
- Dream bigger and do it all again and again and again.

All this leads to Transformation Version 2.0.

TRANSFORMATION IS A PROCESS— NOT A DESTINATION

The good thing about this process is that it works on any scale from small to large. Once you've identified a problem that needs to be solved, put it through the Five Ds process. You can repeat this cycle bigger and better each time you do it. That's how an idea scales and grows. As you repeat the cycle, you'll start to see that your efforts are making a major impact, not just through the numbers and data you collect, but also through the powerful stories of how people's lives are changed because of what you are doing.

We're hoping none of this sounds too complicated. Anyone can discover, design, deploy, document, and dream. You don't have to be part of an organization, be a technical person, or know statistics. If you can observe and ask questions, make a simple plan, follow through on it, check to see if your actions are accomplishing what you had hoped, and then adjust your plan to improve it and make it better, then you can do this.

That's what Missy Hammerstrom did. She was visiting an elementary school in Louisville, Kentucky, for a community project. While she was eating lunch in the cafeteria, a student asked if she could have Missy's apple.

Missy asked if the girl wanted it because she didn't get enough to eat in the lunchroom.

"No," answered the girl. "I'm taking it home so I can eat it tonight."

Naturally, Missy gave the girl her apple. But the experience got her thinking. She realized the kids in the school weren't getting enough to eat at home. That night she told her husband, Gary, she had to do something. She couldn't let kids go home and be hungry, so she formulated a plan. She went to a nearby store to buy backpacks and food. She packed those backpacks with food in her garage and donated them to the girl's school.

With those small steps in 2005 Missy started what turned into Blessings in a Backpack. What began with a few backpacks in a garage has grown into a national organization that's sending

87,300 kids home with food every weekend.[20] In Louisville alone, the organization feeds 5,000 students in 48 schools.[21]

Whether you're trying to make things better in your family, improve your community, or create global initiatives for change, John Doerr's advice to the two college dropouts who created Google apply to us all. If you don't measure what you're doing, you won't be able to get your great idea to give you the results you desire.

I'm personally very thankful to Rob and his team for what I've learned about research and measuring progress. I have become a better leader as a result, and my organizations have become more effective. These lessons will help you too, whether you're leading an organization, as we are, or if you're a parent who got an idea when a child asked for an apple. Anyone can do this. Transformation is within reach of anyone who is willing to change themselves, live good values, value people, and collaborate with others to bring about lasting positive change. That's what the John Maxwell Leadership Foundation is working to do, that's what OneHope is working to do, and it's something you can do too.

CHAPTER 8

LET'S KEEP TALKING

We are today where our conversations have brought us. We will be tomorrow where our conversations take us.

Recently I spoke to a group of about five thousand leaders who work in the nonprofit arena. I was casting vision and talking about what might be accomplished through partnership between my nonprofit organization and theirs. It was a fantastic session. Afterward, I sat in the green room with the top leaders of the hosting organization so we could brainstorm ideas for what we could do together. Even before we could land any definitive plans, Larry Stockstill, who is one of their leaders, said, "John, the answer is yes. Count me in. Whatever this means, I am a yes." His response felt like it paved the way to unlimited possibilities for us, and that got all of us excited.

After the meeting I thanked Larry for his support, and I asked him what made him jump in so boldly.

"I live on the other side of yes," Larry said. "That's where I find abundance and opportunity. It's where I become a better and bigger self. The opportunity of a lifetime must be seized within the lifetime of the opportunity. So I try to say yes whenever I can."

> "THE OPPORTUNITY OF A LIFETIME MUST BE SEIZED WITHIN THE LIFETIME OF THE OPPORTUNITY."
> —LARRY STOCKSTILL

I love Larry's perspective. He *wants* to say yes. He sees life as positive and bursting with possibilities, he is open to them, and he expresses it positively. And because he does, the opportunities flow to him.

COMMUNITY TRANSFORMATION IS A YES CONVERSATION

We need to learn from Larry's example. How we see things determines how we say things, and how we say things always influences—and often determines—how they turn out. If we want to be part of a transformational process or help to contribute to a transformational movement, we need to live on the other side of yes. Here's what we think that means.

LIVING ON THE OTHER SIDE OF YES MEANS BELIEVING IN POSSIBILITIES

When you live on the other side of yes, you believe there is always an answer. In fact, you feel certain there is not just *one* answer; you believe there are many good answers. That makes you willing to do the work to find them, and it also fires you up to be part of them!

Living on the Other Side of Yes Means Having Hope

People who live on the other side of yes find hope in every situation. They believe every person is not only worth helping but actually *can* be helped. And they bring that hope to the people who need it: those who have lost hope, become discouraged, and don't see a positive way forward. Living on the other side of yes is life-giving.

Living on the Other Side of Yes Means Speaking Positively

When you live on the other side of yes, you think and speak positively. You stop asking, "Can we?" and you start asking, "How can we?" Making a difference isn't a matter of if; it's a matter of how and when. And like Larry Stockstill, you use positive words to inspire positive action in others. You empower others with the power of your hope. You use your communication as a catalyst to transform communities.

Keep Talking in a Crisis

Speaking positively and living on the other side of yes can sometimes be challenging, especially in the face of adversity or problems. That was certainly true for Roy Moore, a friend of Rob's. Roy got a call one day out of the blue from the assistant headmaster of his son Matthew's school. Roy was told, "You need to come get Matthew. He wants to end his life."

"I was not prepared for that call," said Roy. "I tell you, there was nothing in my experience that ever remotely made me think that my son would be suicidal."

Matthew was a bright, hopeful, good-looking thirteen-year-old kid with loads of potential and great opportunities ahead of him. The boarding school he was attending was for kids just like him— boys with high potential being prepared to be leaders. Matthew's older brother had gone to that school, and Matthew had even attended a summer program there, which he loved. In fact, his first semester there, he seemed to be thriving. He had made friends, played football, performed on stage, made the academic honor roll, and engaged in community service. To all appearances, he was flourishing. The administration even recognized him as a model of what the school was all about.

Roy immediately flew to the school, picked up Matthew, and took him home. Through many conversations, Roy and his wife, Lisa, learned what had happened. Other boys at the school were targeting him and bullying him because he stood out. Nobody was aware of how difficult life had become for Matthew until one day he told the adult monitor of his residence floor that he didn't want to live anymore. He wanted to walk into the nearby lake and drown himself.

Roy and Lisa jumped into action. They engaged a therapist to work with Matthew and them. They started doing research on suicide prevention. They arranged for Matthew to attend a new school. And they kept talking with him, trying to help him regain the joy and hope he once had in his life. But Roy could tell it wasn't working. After the first day of eighth grade in his new school, Matthew went to the principal's office and said, "I'm not feeling well. I'm not sure I can do this type of thing."

Roy felt like a failure as a parent. "Matthew had been raised with values and the belief that he could accomplish whatever he set his mind to. But I didn't raise him to expect that there would be people in this world who intend you harm."

A LIFELINE FOR MATTHEW

As Roy began to learn about suicide, he discovered that people who take their own lives have the intent to kill themselves, a plan to do it, and a timeframe for following through. One day when Matthew suddenly stopped being agitated and calmly told his mother, "I'm going to miss you," they realized that was where Matthew was. They knew they needed to act. As they searched for a way to help him, they found only one viable option: a residential treatment facility out of state. Immediately the three of them were on their way there. As Matthew was being admitted, it broke Roy's heart to see his son look drawn, his eyes dark and downcast, like someone unable to find his way.

Matthew spent a year in that facility. Roy and Lisa frequently flew back there for sessions with him, sessions on their own with a therapist, and sessions with other parents and their children. "There was a period where he was really working," said Roy, "and then he hit a point of helplessness that lasted for several months. We didn't know if he was going to turn the corner." But, fortunately, Matthew did.

WHERE CAN OTHERS TURN?

During that dark period when Roy and Lisa were at the facility, they heard other families' tragic stories of kids being bullied and wanting to die. Roy started asking broader questions. "How bad is this?" "How big of an issue is this?" "Who's addressing this?" "Why don't more people know that we have over a million of our kids trying to end their lives every year?" "Why didn't I know about that?"

Roy learned that bullying was a huge issue. And it was different from the way it was when he, Rob, or I were kids. Years ago, if you had a problem with a bully at school, you found relief from it when you went home. Now because of communication, cell phones, and social media, being bullied follows you everywhere. That is one of the reasons twenty teenagers take their own lives every day in the United States.

Roy began to research bullying prevention. He looked for organizations that were helping parents like him with this huge problem. But he didn't find a single organization that he believed was doing anything to actually *change* the situation. So he decided to step up and do something about it himself. He dedicated himself to creating the kind of organization that could make a difference for struggling teens.

Roy began with his heart. "I started thinking about the people we would serve," he said. "I wanted to understand what it's like to serve somebody like my son, like these kids, and parents like us. How do you help kids move from victim to victor?"

THE BIRTH OF BE STRONG

Roy knew that teens didn't want to hear a man in his fifties talk about bullying, so he recruited Nick Vujicic to become the main communicator about bullying. But Roy knew that lasting change required more than just anti-bullying messages. What Roy developed was an organization called Be Strong. Its focus was on using positive communication to lessen bullying, help kids overcome bullying when it does happen, and prevent suicides. The organization now does this through what Roy described as four main channels:

- **Hosting Large Events:** What began in auditoriums and arenas has continued with events that are simulcast to large audiences. For example, a single event in Houston in 2019 reached 1.25 million students.

- **Recruiting and Empowering Student Leaders:** Knowing that the most effective conversations are student to student, Be Strong started recruiting and training student leaders to start clubs on school campuses. In those clubs, kids are able to connect with other kids, giving them hope and offering a place to belong. Students are also encouraged to eat lunch with other kids who appear to be isolated.

- **Offering Programs to Students and Administrators:** In addition to the clubs, students, teachers, and administrators are offered training in a twelve-week resiliency program that teaches social and emotional skills to successfully face difficulties. Ashleigh Cromer, the executive director of Be Strong, said, "We can't stop bullying, but we can learn how to navigate it in a healthy manner."[1]

- **Creating an App People Can Use to Find Help:** Be Strong developed an app kids can use to call 911, text or call a counselor when they're in a crisis, and learn about free services in their zip code.

To say this has been successful would be an understatement. As of early 2020, Be Strong had student leaders (called state reps) in forty-eight states. Be Strong Clubs and We Dine Together initiatives have been established in hundreds of schools in thirty-five states. It's incredible to realize all this has been accomplished in just over five years.

Roy has a lot of hope. More important, so does his son,

Matthew—and tens of thousands of other kids who were once discouraged. Matthew is currently finishing his college education. I asked Roy what Matthew now thinks of all that's been done for so many kids across the country, and Roy told me, "He would gladly go through it again knowing what's come out of it."[2] That's an extraordinary perspective from someone who's gone through so much, and it's a testament to his desire to make a difference for others.

TRANSFORMATION CONVERSATIONS

The Law of Communication in *The 17 Indisputable Laws of Teamwork* states interaction fuels action. Without communication, positive change just doesn't happen. If we want to be agents of transformation, we need to keep talking the way Roy Moore did. And we must learn to have transformation conversations with others.

What's sad is that positive conversations are starting to become a lost art. People have become fixated on problems instead of solutions, they talk instead of listen, they rant on social media instead of sitting down at the table together, and they focus on what divides us instead of what could bring us together. But we can change that. Here are some guidelines for having transformation conversations with people.

1. TRANSFORMATION CONVERSATIONS START WITH REALITY

Just because transformation conversations are positive doesn't mean they ignore reality. You don't solve problems by avoiding them or overcome obstacles by pretending they don't exist.

However, not everyone is willing to start the conversation with reality. In his book *Managing in Turbulent Times*, Peter Drucker wrote: "A time of turbulence is a dangerous time, but its greatest danger is a temptation to deny reality."[3] That temptation often comes out in words like these:

- "Let someone else deal with those problems."
- "Those issues will never go away, so why bother."
- "Somebody will do something about that when it gets bad enough."
- "I'll get around to doing something about that eventually."

While others either ignore problems or complain about them, people who work to change their world face up to them and do something. As you get ready to start a transformation conversation, it should sound more like this:

- **"Yes, we have problems."** The process begins with acknowledging, defining, and respecting the problem.
- **"There are answers to this problem."** As we've already pointed out, to be successful, you must believe there are answers before you can find them.
- **"We must be part of these answers."** Roy Moore could have been satisfied with Matthew's recovery and returned back to his own interests. But he didn't. The conversations he had with other families made him aware of two things. First, bullying and its effect on people was a problem bigger than what had happened in his family. This was the reality. Second, he wanted to do something about it.

If we want the problems of our world to change, we need to face reality and become part of the solution. Change begins with you and me when we take action. That doesn't mean there won't be challenges. Everything worthwhile is uphill. The climb may be slow. That's okay. Community transformation isn't easy, but it is always worthwhile.

2. Transformation Conversations Generate Better Ideas and Solutions

When you live on the other side of yes and engage in transformation conversations, it stimulates people to find better answers. When it comes to generating ideas, dialogues are always better than monologues. And polylogues—that's a conversation involving three or more people—are even better. If one person can come up with good ideas, a group can come up with many good ideas. And when you get enough good ideas and enough people working together to improve them, you can generate great ideas.

For many years, my team and I have engaged in transformation conversations to generate better ideas. Every major book I've written has engaged in these creative sessions where the best idea wins—including this book. These were especially fun and productive because both of us had members of our team coming up with ideas. I loved it.

We use transformation conversations to generate ideas and solutions in our organizations too. My CEO Mark Cole and I have had a series of transformational discussions with Richard Chandler and his team. Richard, a very successful businessman and philanthropist, is the chairman of the Clermont Group, a cutting-edge organization that lifts up countries by promoting good business values. He is the one who gave me the idea for the ladder as one of the elements of a movement. That led me to think of ideas for the other five images.

In another example of the kind of synergy that occurs in these transformation conversations, I met with my writing team—Charlie Wetzel, Jason Brooks, and Erin Miller—to talk about the elements in a movement, and everyone latched onto the idea of using images to represent them. Erin, who has helped me with writing our youth curriculum and is very intuitive, shared her insights. And talented Jason started drawing them on a nearby whiteboard. His versions looked very close to the ones we finally used.

Our goal was to make the ideas for the transformational movement simple and sticky. Because we all said, "Let's keep talking," we were able to come up with the images we used and the phrases top-down, bottom-up, inside-out, and so on. Who knows what you will discover, learn, and improve when you value the conversations you have and keep talking.

3. TRANSFORMATION CONVERSATIONS OFFER HOPE

The defining characteristic of any transformation conversation is hope. Without hope, people won't keep working toward transformation. But with it, they will keep striving. Hope is one of the reasons Rob and I wrote this book. We want it to be a message of hope to you so that you can share that message with others.

Notice the contrast between people with low hope and people with high hope:

Low Hope	High Hope
Focus on symptoms	Focus on solutions
Avoid	Engage
Feed fear	Feed faith
Get tired	Get inspired
Drop out	Dive in
Give up	Get going

Hope is uplifting and inspiring, but it's also something more. Psychologist Shane Lopez, who was a senior scientist for Gallup, pointed out the difference between wishful thinking and hope—and how much stronger hope is. "When we hope, we have high expectations for the future *and* a clear-eyed view of the obstacles that we need to overcome in order to get there. We are primed for action. But wishful thinking can undermine our efforts, making us passive and less likely to reach coveted goals."[4] He also pointed to the strength of hope over optimism. He wrote,

> THE DEFINING CHARACTERISTIC OF ANY TRANSFORMATION CONVERSATION IS HOPE.

> You're optimistic if you think the future will be better than the present . . . You're hopeful if you think that the future will be better and you have a role in making it so. You might consider yourself a hard-nosed realist, even a pessimist—someone who

sees the world in a clear, cold light—but you take action to improve any situation that's important to you.

Optimism is an attitude. It doesn't concern itself with real information about the future, and it may not have a specific goal. . . . Optimism is partly based on temperament. . . . But when life throws us a curve, when the going gets tough, optimists can get stuck and frustrated. Hopeful people shine in negative situations. They are energized to act and they find meaning and dignity in moving ahead, whatever the challenge.[5]

This balance—between realistic thinking, the desire for a better future, the energy and will to act, and taking responsibility to create positive change—is powerful. However, the power is released only when that hope is expressed. That was what happened in my interaction with Larry Stockstill that I described in the beginning part of this chapter. When Larry said, "The answer is yes," he was voicing hope *and* his intention to help make what we hoped for a reality. And his expression of hope filled the room with hope, and that is when the conversation became filled with possibility.

Rob speaks highly of the book *Hope Rising* by Casey Gwinn and Chan Hellman and often recommends it. In the book, the authors defined hope this way: "Hope is not just an idea. Hope is not simply an emotion. It is far more than a feeling. It is not a wish or even an expectation. Hope is about goals, willpower, and pathways. A person with high hope has goals, the motivation to pursue them, and the determination to overcome obstacles and find pathways to achieve them."[6] Those are the things you want to include in any transformation conversation you have with others. You want to make the goals clear. You want to harness the collective willpower to achieve those goals, and you want to show people the pathway forward together so that those goals can be achieved. Just as important, you want to be proactive yourself and encourage the person you're talking with to be proactive in taking an active role in bringing what you're hoping for to fruition. As Gwinn and Hellman observed, "Hope is the belief that your future can be brighter

> "HOPEFUL PEOPLE SHINE IN NEGATIVE SITUATIONS."
> —SHANE LOPEZ

and better than your past and that you actually have a role to play in making it better."[7] Rob has read many of the studies that validate the science of hope.[8] They provide further support for what we discussed in the previous chapter on measuring outcomes.

4. TRANSFORMATION CONVERSATIONS CELEBRATE SUCCESSES THROUGH STORYTELLING

One of the most effective means of communication is storytelling. Vanessa Boris, a senior manager at Harvard Business Publishing, observed,

> Telling stories is one of the most powerful means that leaders have to influence, teach, and inspire. What makes storytelling so effective for learning? For starters, storytelling forges connections among people, and between people and ideas. Stories convey the culture, history, and values that unite people. When it comes to our countries, our communities, and our families, we understand intuitively that the stories we hold in common are an important part of the ties that bind.[9]

Rob and I have used storytelling throughout our entire careers. Stories are powerful at every stage of communication—from casting vision to recruiting to training to reinforcing good work to encouraging people when they're down to celebrating victories together.

Why are stories so effective?

Good Stories Move People Emotionally

A well-told story does more than simply convey information or give a chronology of events. It makes use of conflict, tension, or suspense to engage emotion. It includes humor. In short, it has heart. And that's important. When people hear a story, they put themselves into it. That connects them to it personally. One of the most emotionally moving stories people can hear is one about personal transformation. One person's story of positive change becomes a testimony to others about their ability to experience positive change, and it gives them the desire to have their life change too. No wonder people move toward the transformation conversations around them.

Good Stories Communicate Truths

Because stories connect at the emotional level as well as the intellectual level, they can communicate deep truths. Storyteller, poet, and teacher Merna Hecht said, "There is a *tremendous* difference between news and Story. The news media informs the mind—in important ways, I don't deny that. But storytelling is the kind of information that allows *transformation*."[10]

You can journey throughout human history and find that stories have been used to communicate truth. From the earliest times, people gathered around campfires or painted images on cave walls to tell stories. Poets like Homer sang stories like the *Iliad* and the *Odyssey* to convey cultural and societal truths. Jesus told parables to communicate deep spiritual truths. The Brothers Grimm collected folk tales that taught common sense lessons that were passed down from one generation to another. And today filmmakers create movies both fictional and factual to communicate ideas and move people.

The stories I like best are the ones that communicate the truth of positive change real people experience as their lives improve. Here are some stories of change based on the pictures of transformation I shared in chapter 4.

The waterfall represents leaders who pour the waters of transformation out to others, people like Gaby Teasdale from Paraguay. She was inspired to try to bring positive change to her country and became a catalyst for transformation. When she got home from a conference, she started talking to her family, community members, and leaders about the possibilities of making a difference there. Remarkably, without any direct connections to the president of Paraguay, she was able to speak with him and get him on board with the process of teaching and practicing good values in transformation tables. Thanks to her, 247,000 people are participating in transformation tables today. And thousands of students are learning values from the iLead program in schools.

The ladder is a picture of hope, a way for people to climb out of poverty and live the life of their dreams. Yomila Cos from Guatemala has been climbing that ladder. She said,

> I used to be very shy and fearful. I felt afraid of meeting new people and experiencing new things. Participating in a values roundtable was very helpful to me. I got to meet new people and spend time with them. It was a great opportunity for my life.

The value of attitude had the greatest impact on me. It made me realize everything that I was missing out on and helped me see the opportunities that life was presenting me. At that time, I was offered a job opportunity that in previous months I would have rejected out of fear. But I had made the decision to change my attitude, so I took the chance and accepted the job. That decision opened up a whole new world for me! My work has allowed me to positively influence surrounding villages. None of this would have happened had I not made the decision to change my attitude.

Yomila is now climbing the ladder of hope and building ladders for others in her community.

The heart represents change from the inside-out when people learn and live good values. Deborah Sandoval, a police officer in Guatemala, experienced that kind of change in her life when she adopted the value of listening. She said, "I'm in the process of learning to listen more to avoid misunderstandings at home and at work. I used to interrupt people when they spoke. I would regularly finish their sentences, but most of the time I was wrong or misinterpreted what they were trying to say. The first one to notice my change was my husband, and our relationship has improved tremendously. The first time I let my husband speak without interrupting, and he noticed it, he almost stopped the car and asked me if I was sick! At that moment I realized how not listening had become an issue in our relationship."

The joined hands tell the story of partnership, like the one between my nonprofit organization EQUIP with Lidere when we launched the Million Leaders Mandate. As we prepared to train leaders in Latin America, I asked John Vereecken, the director of

Lidere, to lead the initiative. Thanks to his leadership and network, together we were able to train half a million leaders in the Spanish-speaking world.

When my nonprofit organizations prepared to launch transformation tables, we partnered with John and Lidere once again. Since 2013 we've launched transformation initiatives in Guatemala, Paraguay, and Costa Rica. More than one and a half million adults and students are learning and living values thanks to that partnership. And Lidere is helping us as we expand our reach outside of Latin America.

Finally, the bridge represents stories of people crossing over from their old way of life to the life they want to live. Morenike Ayinde has introduced an online version of the iChoose curriculum from our iLead program to students in Nigeria and Kenya, and already she is seeing positive changes in students there. A student named Victoria said she has become more positive with others, more intentional in her growth, and more consistent in her daily routine. "I have become more accountable to myself and others, and now I'm very conscious of how I speak to myself and view myself." And Bernice said, "After the lesson on attitude, I started a gratitude journal. It helps me list the things I'm grateful for."

The progress Morenike has seen in others inspires her to keep working. She knows what she's doing is working, because of the stories she hears. She said, "My dream is to raise and equip the next generation of leaders across Africa." She is doing what she can to change her world.

Good Stories Stick with People

Stories also help people to remember what they've learned. They're sticky. That's one of the reasons I've always told stories in my books. Facts fade, but stories stick with people. When they embrace the story, even if they've forgotten the facts, the story can lead them back to the truth contained within it.

Research bears this out. Experts have found that when people hear stories, the pleasurable hormone oxytocin—called the cuddle or holiday hormone—is released. No wonder Jennifer Aaker, General Atlantic Professor of Marketing at Stanford University's Graduate School of Business, found that stories are remembered up to twenty-two times more than facts alone.[11] If you want people to remember what you communicate in a transformation conversation, include a story.

Good Stories Inspire Others

When we launch a new transformation initiative in a country, I invite coaches from the John Maxwell Team to join me to train people in how to do transformation tables. Hundreds excitedly volunteer, pay their own way, and become part of the launch.

The first night there, I bring all of them together to tell them a story—a story about themselves to inspire them. I say, "Your life is about to change in a wonderful way. You are going to go out to businesses, government offices, and schools to train facilitators of transformation tables. Over the next three days we will equip ten thousand people! You've given up a lot to be here in your time and money. And you will work hard. But you will add value to people. And you will make a difference.

"Other teams like this one have preceded you," I continue. "They all have experienced what you are about to discover. Your sacrifice will turn into significance. No matter how much you give, you will receive back more. No matter how much you teach, you will learn more. No matter how much you love, you will receive more. You came to make a positive difference in the lives of others. You will leave knowing that others made a positive difference in you. Once you have experienced significance, success will never satisfy you again."

At the end of those three grueling days where the coaches spend hours traveling by car or van, often over difficult roads, and spend hours training others through inexperienced translators, we gather back together to talk about the experience. And we tell stories. We laugh, we cry, and we celebrate. It's such an inspiration that many of our coaches volunteer again the next time we do an overseas training.

When people know their efforts are actually coming to fruition and transformation is occurring, it inspires them to keep working. Michael Margolis, the CEO of Get Storied, said, "The stories we tell literally make the world. If you want to change the world, you need to change your story. This truth applies both to individuals and institutions."[12] When you become transformed, you change your story. When you tell that story of transformation in a conversation, you help others to begin, embrace, or sustain their own transformation. And as they change, they can help others change. That's how we change the world.

5. TRANSFORMATION CONVERSATIONS PROVIDE A SUPPORTIVE COMMUNITY

When people get together and have honest conversations about their transformation, they create a supportive community for one another. That's one of the reasons transformation tables are so effective. People can encourage one another and express belief in their ability to change. They can engage in tough conversations when needed. The people who are ahead in the process can mentor the others who are not as far along in the journey. It is obvious that time around the table with others helps in a way that couldn't happen with individuals on their own.

6. TRANSFORMATION CONVERSATIONS ACTIVATE PEOPLE'S POTENTIAL

What is the highest goal of a transformation conversation? It's to activate the potential in others. When we believe in people, support them, challenge them, bring out their best, speak the truth to them, and inspire them, we help them to be their best selves. That requires them not only to change but to change into the people they always *could* be.

That happened to Rob in 1995 when he experienced a transformational conversation that changed the course of his life. At that time, Rob was considering a career transition. For years he had worked under his father's leadership at OneHope. Being part of a nonprofit is wonderful in many ways, but it also has its own unique challenges. Rob was ready to step away from OneHope in order to take a stable and lucrative position in business. But then his dad, Bob, was diagnosed with stage-four cancer.

> WHAT IS THE HIGHEST GOAL OF A TRANSFORMATION CONVERSATION? IT'S TO ACTIVATE THE POTENTIAL IN OTHERS.

Stage-four cancer is not a diagnosis anyone wants to get, because the prognosis usually isn't good. While Bob was convalescing, Rob was asked to take his father's place in the organization. So he found himself wrestling with the decision about whether to leave, while at the same time stepping up to take on more responsibility.

One of the tasks Rob had to take on immediately was attending a conference. It was a very high priority to his dad, but Rob didn't want to go. He was feeling crushed under the new pressure of leading OneHope. He felt inadequate to fill his father's accomplished shoes. And he was behind on his work. "I felt insecure and, frankly, like a failure," Rob said. But seeing no other options, Rob hopped on a plane and went.

Since he couldn't avoid the conference, Rob's strategy was to get a room by himself so he could get as much work done as possible. But there was a problem. When he arrived at the conference center, he learned that an acquaintance, Morgan Jackson, had requested they room together, and there were no other options for Rob.

During the conference, Rob attended several meetings, most of which he considered a waste of time. *Why am I here?* he wondered. When he could, he retreated to his room to work. But Jackson, who was also the director of a nonprofit organization, was often there. And he was a talker. Every time Rob sat down to work or tried to go to sleep, Jackson started talking. One of their conversations ended up being life changing. Rob said,

Jackson said that he was in a similar position to me. He had taken over a nonprofit from his father too. And he felt like an utter failure. He couldn't do what his dad had done, and he planned to quit.

Jackson said he took a walk in a garden one afternoon, where he saw a mix of exotic plants, many of which were in pots everywhere. When he spotted the gardener, he asked him, "Why do you have all these potted plants?"

"These are plants that we sell," responded the gardener. "Can you guess how old these are?"

Jackson looked at the potted plants and took a guess. "I don't know. A couple of months old?"

"No," the gardener responded. "They are anywhere from three to five years old." Then he pointed to several large trees in the garden, laden with fruit. "How old do you think these are?"

"Ten years?" Jackson guessed.

"They're the same age: three to five years. The difference between them is that those are potted," he said pointing to the smaller plants, "and these are planted," he said pointing to the large healthy one.

Jackson finally said to me, "Rob, God told me to ask you a question: Are you potted or planted?"

That conversation was truly transformational for Rob. He wrestled with that question. Was he potted or planted? After hours of thinking and praying, Rob made a decision. He wanted to have a fruitful life.

"I planted myself in the vision, even with all of my insecurities, with all of my fears," said Rob. "If the winds blew, if the storms came, if Dad died, it didn't matter. I was committed. I didn't want to live a potted life."

When Rob returned home, he found that his was recovering. Bob is still alive and well more than twenty-five years later. And Rob is still planted firmly in the vision of OneHope.

· · ·

Perhaps that is the greatest value of transformational conversations. They move us to make better decisions that better ourselves and others. Transformational conversations inspire what's next.

They make us intentional. They encourage us to live a planted life instead of a potted one.

Are you willing to engage in transformational conversations both as the inspirer and the inspired, as the mentor and the mentored, as the storyteller and the listener, as the team builder and the team member? Are you willing to keep talking so that everyone will keep doing? We hope and believe your answer is yes. If you haven't already begun to connect with others and have transformational conversations, start today. Help others reach their potential. It will make their lives richer and help both you and them to be part of the transformational movements that change the world.

CHAPTER 9

IT'S YOUR TURN TO CHANGE YOUR WORLD

They always say that time changes things, but
you actually have to change them yourself.
—ANDY WARHOL

As you begin to read this final chapter of *Change Your World*, you may be working out how to put all this together. Perhaps you've already begun. If so, we want to encourage you and support you. But we also want to offer you a clear way forward so you can take your turn changing your world.

FOLLOW THE MAP

We have given you a road map for transformation. The very first thing we asked you in chapter 1 was whether you wanted to change your world, change yourself, and become part of a transformational movement. Our desire has been for the chapters of this book to take you on an aspirational journey in four phases, from me to we to making a difference together. This is a model of transformational change that Rob and I have experienced. It looks like this:

PHASE 1	PHASE 2	PHASE 3	PHASE 4	TRANSFORMATION
I Want to Make a Difference	With People Who Make a Difference	Living Values That Make a Difference	Taking Action That Makes a Difference	Your World Changes

Each phase of the journey represents growth and expansion for anyone who wants to change their world.

Phase 1: I Want to Make a Difference

The first two chapters, "We Can't Wait for Change" and "Become a Catalyst for Change," were all about the desire to make a difference. We hope that reading them fed a growing passion within you to change your world, and affirmed your ability to make a difference. We've done our best to water the seeds of compassion and conviction in you so that they would blossom into hope, hope that can now be harnessed to make your world a better place. You've experienced the stories of individuals who made a difference, many of them unsuspecting that they would ever effect such great change. You've discovered that the catalysts of change in our world are often common people, fueled by discontent, frustration, or anger, who channeled their emotions into doing good. Their actions first produced a change in themselves, and out of that change they added amazing value to others, became leaders, and initiated transformational movements.

PHASE 2: WITH PEOPLE WHO MAKE A DIFFERENCE

In chapters 3 and 4, "We All Need One Another" and "Let's All Get on the Same Page," we presented the idea that change is greater when everyone works together, each person bringing specific skills, talent, and experience to the table to make everyone better. When people collaborate, movements often start. As a result, transformation often occurs on a greater scale, positively impacting more people and making a greater difference. As we explored why some movements succeed while others fail, the stories all had one thing in common: when people who care get on the same page and work from a foundation of shared values, they can make a difference.

PHASE 3: LIVING VALUES THAT MAKE A DIFFERENCE

Rob and I have never seen positive change occur or the transformation of a community happen unless good values were embraced by the people involved. We hope the stories of life change in chapter 5, "Experience the Value of Values," helped you embrace the power of values to change anyone's life. Whatever your hopes and dreams for positive change—for yourself or others—living good values will expand them. Good values always make a difference.

Through years of helping people and adding value to them, we've discovered the best way to help people live good values is through transformation tables. That's why we told you about them and how they work in chapter 6, "Transformation Happens One Table at a Time."

Phase 4: Taking Action That Makes a Difference

Chapters 7 and 8, "What Gets Done Gets Measured" and "Let's Keep Talking," were all about taking action. In them we offered practical principles to ensure the action you take creates the difference you desire. Hope, though powerful, is not enough to change your world. Action is what actually *makes* the difference. And to keep making a difference, we need to continue talking to one another, to have ongoing transformational conversations.

> HOPE, THOUGH POWERFUL, IS NOT ENOUGH TO CHANGE YOUR WORLD. ACTION IS WHAT ACTUALLY *MAKES* THE DIFFERENCE.

Get in Where You Fit In

Our invitation to you is to follow the road map. We have created one easy way for you to do that through our website ChangeYourWorld.com. This resource-rich platform provides all the tools necessary for you to grow through every phase of the world-changing process. Of course, not everyone will enter using the same on-ramp to transformation. Each of use takes a unique route, but the result we desire is the same. What's important is that you be on the journey. It matters less *how* you get started than that you simply get started.

You May Blaze Your Own Trail

Maybe your journey will be like that of Charlee Tchividjian-Sherry. When she was a junior in high school, she decided to drop out. Her dad, one of Rob's good friends, made it clear to Charlee that if she wasn't going to stay in school, she had to get a job. Rob suggested that Charlee do an internship with OneHope. The idea appealed to her, so she spent five months in South Africa and worked in some of the most poverty-stricken areas of the country.

Her life was changed one day when she was working with children in the slums. A newborn baby was placed into her arms. When she learned the baby had been rescued from the trash because her mother was young and had no support, Charlee was crushed. "I went back to our host home that night and wept. As my tears began to dry, I realized that if just one person had walked alongside that mom in her distress, that child could still have a mother." In that moment, she decided she would do something to help mothers and children. She later said, "I came home from Africa a totally, radically changed person."

Charlee was determined to start a maternity home in Africa right away, but friends and family encouraged her to get a college degree first. So she enrolled at Liberty University in Lynchburg, Virginia. While studying there, she began volunteering with a university program that worked with children in the inner city. She was surprised to find that parts of Lynchburg were at a poverty level similar to parts of Africa. Her heart started to draw her in a new direction. Instead of traveling halfway around the world to help people, she decided to start a support group for the struggling young moms there in Lynchburg, calling it Ēma, which stands for Every Mother's Advocate. What began as a single neighborhood support group soon grew into a bunch of groups in poor neighborhoods throughout the city.

After graduating and getting married, Charlee and her husband, Matt, relocated to South Florida, and she decided to continue Ēma in her new location. True, she would have to start over from scratch, but she was committed to make it happen. However, she questioned whether she was making a positive difference.

After a year of what she said felt like spinning her wheels in mud, she considered quitting. But before that, she decided to take a cold, hard look at what had worked and what had not. Ēma had mentored seventy moms in the area the previous year, and a shockingly high 98 percent had been able to keep their children out of foster care and in their own homes. Charlee knew that every year in South Florida, twenty-four hundred children were placed in foster care.[1] Finally, Charlee had discovered where she could make the biggest difference. She restructured Ēma and put its focus on reducing the number of children in foster care by educating struggling moms and advocating for those in crisis.

Referrals started flowing in. Many of the people Charlee and Ēma helped were like Sarina. When she came to Ēma, Sarina was six months pregnant and living in her broken-down car, which was parked behind a restaurant. Having already lost custody of her two older children, she was desperate for help. Ēma helped her find a place to live, arranged to have her first six months' rent paid, found a mechanic to repair her car at no cost, and helped her find a job. They also counseled and coached her during a traumatic time. And after her son was born, they were her advocates with the court, which allowed her to keep her baby boy.

In its first year with the new focus, Ēma reached 269 mothers and children through its programs and kept 96 children out of foster care. And with an idea expressed by Nelson Mandela ringing in her ears—"If you want the cooperation of humans around you, you must make them feel they are important"—Charlee made sure every young mom who walked through Ēma's doors was treated with dignity, respect, and kindness.

> "IF YOU WANT THE COOPERATION OF HUMANS AROUND YOU, YOU MUST MAKE THEM FEEL THEY ARE IMPORTANT."
> —NELSON MANDELA

Charlee is just a regular person, but she is changing her world by helping moms like Sarina and her son, Jacob. When Charlee got started, she simply followed her heart and took action on what she thought was right. She has blazed her own trail, feeling her way along as she found the place where she could make the most difference. What she has done, you can do. Her greatest strengths were wanting to make a difference, getting started, and persevering. If your path is like hers, then Rob and I are cheering you on!

YOU CAN JOIN OUR TRANSFORMATION TEAM

But maybe you are looking for an existing path to follow. Maybe you feel the pull to make a difference by joining in what Rob and I are doing to change the world. That's what Becky Bursell has done. She has been facilitating transformation tables for the JMLF, and it has changed her life.

Becky is a highly gifted leader and businessperson. For twelve years she and her husband, John, worked with a nutritional supplement company, and they were highly successful. They built an organization of eight hundred thousand sales reps in more than sixty countries. They sold more than a *billion* dollars in products. But at the pinnacle of her success, Becky realized she didn't feel fulfilled. "We've all heard that money doesn't buy happiness," she said. "Well, I had spent twelve years trying to prove that theory wrong. But guess what? Turns out, the saying holds true. How was it that after accomplishing every business and financial goal I had ever set for myself, I was still looking for something greater?"

Becky started searching for answers. "I found myself at forty-one years old having to reevaluate and redefine my values, based on who I wanted to be, not what I wanted in return. The only way for me to do that was to start at the beginning—with a clean slate." She sold her business, reexamined her values, confirmed that she wanted to make a difference in the lives of others, and began searching for a way to do it.

This occurred a decade and a half after I had met Becky. She had read some of my books, and we connected at an event, getting to know each other over lunch. When she told me that she had sold her business and expressed the desire to change her world, I invited her to begin leading transformation tables. It didn't take her long to see how helping others live good values aligned with her extraordinary team-building talent. Becky said, "John's dream of changing the world moved from his dream, to my dream. I realized the value I could bring that no one else could, and we got to work."

Becky immediately appreciated that the materials were already written and ready for anyone who wanted to use them. She began using them herself and soon started training others to use them. She enjoys telling others,

> You can change your world when you . . .
> 1. Facilitate transformation tables.
> 2. Complete the curriculum.
> 3. Live the values.
> 4. Share your experience of transformation.
> 5. Invite others to facilitate transformation tables.
> 6. Repeat.
> This curriculum is so powerful. These are values, embedded in universal principles, that can be applied to every path in life. All we have to do is be the facilitators.

Becky is using the same skills she used in business to make a difference in her community. We can't begin to count the number of people she's trained to facilitate transformation tables. She said, "I've met with business owners, pastors, counselors, corporate executives, government officials, real estate teams, parents, charity organizers—all of them now using transformation tables within their organizations and witnessing thousands of life-changing transformations for themselves."[2]

TAKE YOUR NEXT STEP

What step will *you* take to change your world? Where can you help other people and make a difference? Remember, you don't need to worry about changing the *whole* world. If you can just make things better for *someone* in *your* world, you will experience the reality, joy, and satisfaction of making a difference.

If you want to watch people transform through the power of values in action in their lives, we would love for you to join us, as Becky did, in leading transformation tables. Whether you're a young person just getting started or a seasoned leader who wants to grow their influence and the scope of what you're doing, they will help you make a difference. Our desire isn't to put you into our mold or Becky's or anyone else's. In fact, one of the things Becky told us was this: "These values are allowing me to become the greatest version of me, in a direction that I was already moving toward."

If you have a sense of what you should do, then do it. You can change your world. Remember, transformation is possible for anyone willing to learn and live good values, value people, and collaborate with them to create a positive values culture. Your story can be as powerful as any of the ones we shared with you in this book. What matters now is that you *do* something. Get started today and find out where it leads. Even if it turns out totally different from what you expect, you'll enjoy the journey and you'll never regret working to make a difference, because it will change your world—and you.

Go to ChangeYourWorld.com to receive

- Materials to lead transformation tables
- iLead youth materials
- Information on becoming a part of a transformation team

Notes

Chapter 1: We Can't Wait for Change

1. "Parenting in America," Pew Research Center, Social and Demographic Trends, December 17, 2015, https://www.pewsocialtrends.org/2015/12/17/parenting-in-america/#fn-21212-1.
2. "The Population of Poverty USA," Poverty USA, https://www.povertyusa.org/facts, retrieved September 17, 2019.
3. Robert Putnam, *Bowling Alone: The Collapse and Revival of American Community* (New York: Simon & Schuster, 2000).
4. "Criminal Victimization, 2018, Summary," Bureau of Justice Statistics, Report NCJ 253043, September 2019, https://www.bjs.gov/content/pub/pdf/cv18_sum.pdf.
5. The Chandler Foundation, "Prosperity: A Total Game Approach," *Building a Better World*, October 2019, 21.
6. "Mental Health by the Numbers," National Alliance on Mental Illness, https://www.nami.org/learn-more/mental-health-by-the-numbers, retrieved September 17, 2019.
7. Rachel Schraer, "Is Young People's Mental Health Getting Worse?" BBC News, February 11, 2019, https://www.bbc.com/news/health-47133338.
8. Chandler Foundation, "Prosperity," 27–28.
9. "40 million in modern slavery and 152 million in child labour around the world," International Labour Organization, September

19, 2017, https://www.ilo.org/global/about-the-ilo/newsroom/news
/WCMS_574717/lang—en/index.htm.

10. Max Roser and Esteban Ortiz-Ospina, "Global Extreme Poverty,"
Our World in Data, March 27, 2017, https://ourworldindata.org
/extreme-poverty.

11. Homi Kharas and Kristofer Hamel, "A Global Tipping Point:
Half the World Is Now Middle Class or Wealthier," Brookings,
September 27, 2018, https://www.brookings.edu/blog/future
-development/2018/09/27/a-global-tipping-point-half-the-world
-is-now-middle-class-or-wealthier.

12. Rosamund Stone Zander and Benjamin Zander, *The Art of
Possibility: Transforming Professional and Personal Life* (New York:
Penguin, 2002), 14–15.

13. Jonathan Sacks, The Dignity of Difference: How to Avoid the
Clash of Civilizations (New York: Continuum, 2002), 206.

14. Ellen J. Langer, *Counter Clockwise: Mindful Health and the Power
of Possibility* (New York: Ballantine, 2009), 107.

15. Brad Montague (@KidPresident), Facebook (post), December 12,
2016, https://www.facebook.com/KidPresident/photos/dare-to
-dream-but-please-also-do-for-dreamers-are-many-but-doers-are
-few-a-tiny-/781163668690950.

16. "Our Purpose," Lonesome Dove Ranch, accessed January 13,
2020, http://lonesomedovetexas.com/purpose/.

17. Ed Stetzer, "One-on-One with Bryan Jarrett, on Resourcing
Rural America, Part 2," *Christianity Today*, November 14, 2019,
https://www.christianitytoday.com/edstetzer/2019/november/one
-on-one-with-bryan-jarrett-part-2.html.

18. Stetzer, "One-on-One with Bryan Jarrett."

19. Stetzer, "One-on-One with Bryan Jarrett."

20. Stetzer, "One-on-One with Bryan Jarrett."

21. "Our Purpose," Lonesome Dove Ranch.

22. Chandler Foundation, "Prosperity: A Total Game Approach, 19.

23. Clayton M. Christensen, Efosa Ojomo, and Karen Dillon, *The Prosperity Paradox: How Innovation Can Lift Nations Out of Poverty* (New York: Harper Business, 2019), 6–7.

24. Quoted in "Are You a Reluctant Adapter?" Oprah.com, , accessed January 13, 2020, http://www.oprah.com/inspiration/what-to-do -if-you-hate-change.

25. "Partner," WorldWithoutOrphans.org, accessed March 25, 2020, https://www.worldwithoutorphans.org/partner.

26. "Partner," WorldWithoutOrphans.org.

27. Rob Llewellyn, "20 Ways to Create a Sense of Urgency," The Enterprisers Project, September 24, 2015, https://enterprisers project.com/article/2014/8/20-ways-create-sense-urgency.

28. Loren Eiseley, *The Unexpected Universe* (Orlando: Harvest, 1969).

29. Brené Brown, *Dare to Lead: Brave Work. Tough Conversations. Whole Hearts.* (New York: Random House, 2018), 6.

30. Malcolm Gladwell, "18 Quotes from Malcolm Gladwell's Inbound 2014 Keynote 'The Power of the Underdog,'" SlideShare, September 18, 2014, https://www.slideshare.net /kelseylibert/malcolm-gladwell-39255392.

31. "How Does Level of Education Relate to Poverty?" Center for Poverty Research, University of California, Davis, accessed April 27, 2020, https://poverty.ucdavis.edu/faq/how-does-level -education-relate-poverty.

32. Donald J. Hernandez, "Double Jeopardy: How Third-Grade Reading Skills and Poverty Influence High School Graduation," The Annie E. Casey Foundation, 2012, https://www.aecf.org/m/resourcedoc/AECF-DoubleJeopardy -2012-Full.pdf#page=4.

CHAPTER 2: BECOME A CATALYST FOR CHANGE

1. "Iowa Rep. Tom Latham Pays Tribute to Dr. Borlaug," The World Food Prize, March 20, 2008, https://web.archive.org/web

/20080703155602/http://www.worldfoodprize.org/press_room
/2008/march/latham_borlaug.htm.

2. Mark Stuertz, "Green Giant," *Dallas Observer*, December 5, 2002, https://www.dallasobserver.com/news/green-giant -6389547.

3. Justin Gillis, "Norman Borlaug, Plant Scientist Who Fought Famine, Dies at 95," *New York Times*, September 13, 2009, https://www.nytimes.com/2009/09/14/business/energy -environment/14borlaug.html.

4. Charles C. Mann, "The Book That Incited a Worldwide Fear of Overpopulation," *Smithsonian Magazine*, January 2018, https:// www.smithsonianmag.com/innovation/book-incited-worldwide -fear-overpopulation-180967499/.

5. Clyde Haberman, "The Unrealized Horrors of Population Explosion," *New York Times*, May 31, 2015, https://www.nytimes .com/2015/06/01/us/the-unrealized-horrors-of-population -explosion.html.

6. Gillis, "Norman Borlaug."

7. Gillis, "Norman Borlaug."

8. Gillis, "Norman Borlaug."

9. Aase Lionæs, "Award Ceremony Speech," The Nobel Peace Prize 1970, accessed January 14, 2020, https://www.nobelprize.org /prizes/peace/1970/ceremony-speech/.

10. In George Sweeting, *Who Said That? More than 2,500 Usable Quotes and Illustrations* (Chicago: Moody, 1995), 4780 of 7400, Kindle.

11. Zechariah 4:10 NLT.

12. William A. Cohen, *Drucker on Leadership: New Lessons from the Father of Modern Management* (San Francisco: Jossey-Bass, 2010), 8 of 292, Kindle.

13. Hans Rosling, with Ola Rosling and Anna Rosling Rönnlund, *Factfulness: Ten Reasons We're Wrong About the World—and Why*

Things Are Better Than You Think (New York: Flatiron Books, 2018), 69–71.

14. Greg Braxton, "Take a Tour of Tyler Perry's Massive New Studio on a Former Army Base in Atlanta," *Lost Angeles Times*, October 13, 2016, https://www.latimes.com/entertainment/tv/la-ca-st-tyler -perry-guided-tour-20161016-snap-story.html.

15. "Tyler Perry: Biography," IMDb.com, accessed January 16, 2020, https://www.imdb.com/name/nm1347153/bio?ref_=nm_ov_bio_sm.

16. "Tyler Perry Studios," Tyler Perry Studios, accessed January 16, 2020, https://tylerperrystudios.com.

17. Brian MacQuarrie, "Malala Yousafzai Addresses Harvard Audience," *Boston Globe*, September 27, 2013, https://www .bostonglobe.com/metro/2013/09/27/malala-yousafzai-pakistani -teen-shot-taliban-tells-harvard-audience-that-education-right-for -all/6cZBan0M4J3cAnmRZLfUmI/story.html.

18. Martin Luther King Jr., "'Desegregation and the Future,' Address Delivered at the Annual Luncheon of the National Committee for Rural Schools," New York, NY, December 15, 1956, https:// kinginstitute.stanford.edu/king-papers/documents/desegregation -and-future-address-delivered-annual-luncheon-national -committee.

19. "Take the Pledge," Operation Change, accessed June 16, 2020, https://www.operationchange.com/pledge.

20. Benjamin Hardy, "If You're Going to Do Something, See How Far You Can Go," Benjamin Hardy's Blog, March 16, 2019, https://www.goodreads.com/author_blog_posts/18093140-if-you -re-going-to-do-something-see-how-far-you-can-go.

21. "About Us," Maria Cristina Foundation, accessed January 17, 2020, https://mariacristinafoundation.org/maria-conceicao/.

22. "How Maria Conceicao Went from Poverty to Alleviating It," Swaay, https://www.swaay.com/maria-conceicao, accessed January 17, 2020.

23. "How Maria Conceicao Went from Poverty to Alleviating It," Swaay, https://www.swaay.com/maria-conceicao.
24. Farah Andrews, "How Maria Conceicao Plans to Swim the English Channel to Raise Awareness for Slum Kids," The National, August 20, 2019, https://www.thenational .ae/lifestyle/how-maria-conceicao-plans-to-swim-the-english-channel-to-raise-awareness-for-slum-kids-1.900441.
25. "About Us," Maria Cristina Foundation.
26. Sangeetha Swaroop, "Maria Conceicao: I Climbed Mt Everest for the Slum Children," Friday Magazine, August 16, 2013, https:// fridaymagazine.ae/life-culture/maria-conceicao-i-climbed-mt -everest-for-the-slum-children-1.1220821.
27. "How Maria Conceicao Went from Poverty to Alleviating It," Swaay, https://www.swaay.com/maria-conceicao.
28. Swaroop, "Maria Conceicao."
29. Search results for "Maria Conceicao," Guinness World Records, accessed April 27, 2020, https://www.guinnessworldrecords.com /search?term=Maria%20Conceicao&page=1&type=all&max=20 &partial=_Results&.
30. "How Maria Conceicao Went from Poverty to Alleviating It," Swaay, https://www.swaay.com/maria-conceicao.
31. "How Maria Conceicao Went from Poverty to Alleviating It," Swaay, https://www.swaay.com/maria-conceicao.

Chapter 3: We All Need One Another

1. "Top 110 Mother Teresa Quotes and Sayings on Love and Life," Quote Ambition, accessed April 10, 2020, http://www.quoteambition.com/mother-teresa-quotes -sayings.
2. "WHO Announces COVID-19 Outbreak a Pandemic," World Health Organization, Regional Office for Europe, March 12, 2020, http://www.euro.who.int/en/health-topics/health

-emergencies/coronavirus-covid-19/news/news/2020/3/who
-announces-covid-19-outbreak-a-pandemic.

3. Email from Sam Yoder to author, April 7, 2020.

4. Dave Mast, "Nonessential? Not Berlin Gardens as company produces face guards," The Bargain Hunter, April 4, 2020, https://thebargainhunter.com/news/features/nonessential-not -berlin-gardens-as-local-company-produces-face-guards-to -combat-covid-19.

5. Elizabeth Williamson, "In Ohio, the Amish Take On the Coronavirus," New York Times, April 9, 2020, https://www.nytimes .com/2020/04/09/us/politics/amish-coronavirus-ohio.html.

6. Reid Hoffman and Ben Casnocha, The Start-Up of You: Adapt to the Future, Invest in Yourself, and Transform Your Career (New York: Currency, 2012), 83, Kindle.

7. Gustavo Razzetti, "You Don't Need to Change the World Alone: Find Your Partner in Crime," Psychology Today, September 21, 2018, https://www.psychologytoday.com/us/blog/the-adaptive -mind/201809/you-dont-need-change-the-world-alone?amp.

8. Richard Barrett, "Liberating the Corporate Soul: Building a High-Performance, Values-Driven Organization," in The Workplace and Spirituality: New Perspectives on Research and Practice, ed. Joan Marques, Satinder Dhiman, and Richard King (Woodstock, VT: Skylight Paths, 2009), 149–150.

9. P. B. S. Lissaman and Carl A. Shollenberger, "Formation Flight of Birds," Science 168, no. 3934 (May, 1970): 1003–1005, https://doi. org/10.1126/science.168.3934.1003.

10. Charles R. Swindoll, "No Place for Islands," Insight, June 21, 2017, https://www.insight.org/resources/daily-devotional /individual/no-place-for-islands.

11. Theodore Roosevelt, Speech at the Sorbonne, Paris, April 23, 1910, quoted by Christen Duxbury, "It Is Not the Critic Who Counts," January 18, 2011, Theodore Roosevelt Conservation

Partnership, https://www.trcp.org/2011/01/18/it-is-not-the-critic-who-counts.

12. Brené Brown, *Daring Greatly: How the Courage to Be Vulnerable Transforms the Way We Live, Love, Parent, and Lead* (New York: Avery, 2012), 71, Kindle.

13. Gardiner Morse, "The Science Behind Six Degrees," *Harvard Business Review*, February 2003, https://hbr.org/2003/02/the-science-behind-six-degrees.

14. Aimee Groth, "Scientists Reveal the 'Tipping Point' for Ideas Is When There's a 10% Consensus," Business Insider, July 27, 2011, https://www.businessinsider.com/scientists-reveal-the-tipping-point-for-ideas-is-when-theres-a-10-consensus-2011–7.

15. Bettie Marlowe, "Donkeys Kick Each Other. . .," *Cleveland Daily Banner*, May 5, 2017, http://clevelandbanner.com/stories/donkeys-kick-each-other,57996.

16. John F. Kenndy, "Inaugural Address," 44th presidential inauguration, Washington, D.C., January 20, 1961, https://avalon.law.yale.edu/20th_century/kennedy.asp.

17. Edwin Markham, "A Creed to Mr. David Lubin," in *Lincoln and Other Poems* (New York: McClure, Phillips, 1901), 25.

18. "Rocky Quotes," IMDb.com, accessed June 16, 2020, https://www.imdb.com/title/tt0075148/quotes?ref_=tt_ql_trv_4.

19. Melissa Breyer, "11 Facts About Coast Redwoods, The Tallest Trees in the World," Treehugger, September 26, 2019, (updated May 21, 2020), https://www.treehugger.com/natural-sciences/11-facts-about-coast-redwoods-worlds-tallest-trees.html.

20. Greg Satell, *Cascades: How to Create a Movement That Drives Transformational Change* (New York: McGraw-Hill Education, 2019), 98.

21. "List of Marchers Who Participated in the 1930 Dandi March," Dandi Memorial, accessed April 10, 2020, http://www.dandimemorial.in/pdf/List-of-1930-Salt-Marchers.pdf.

22. Evan Andrews, "When Gandhi's Salt March Rattled British Colonial Rule," History, October 2, 2019, https://www.history .com/news/gandhi-salt-march-india-british-colonial-rule.

23. Vincent van Gogh to Theo van Gogh, October 22, 1882, Vincent van Gogh Letters, Letter no. 274, Van Gogh Museum of Amsterdam, http://vangoghletters.org/vg/letters/let274/letter.html.

24. Gina Pogol, "How Long Does It Take to Close on a House?" The Mortgage Reports, July 26, 2019, https://themortgagereports.com /19487/how-long-does-it-take-to-close-a-mortgage-gina-pogol.

25. "Our Story," Movement Mortgage, accessed April 14, 2020, https://movement.com/about-us.

26. "Our Story," Movement Mortgage.

27. "Casey Crawford Receives John Maxwell Transformational Leadership Award," Cision PR Newswire, August 7, 2018, https://www.prnewswire.com/news-releases/casey-crawford -receives-john-maxwell-transformational-leadership-award -300693213.html.

28. Patricia Fripp, "A Team Is More than a Group of People," Fripp, January 23, 2009, https://www.fripp.com/a-team-is-more-than -a-group-of-people.

Chapter 4: Let's All Get on the Same Page

1. Mattathias Schwartz, "Pre-Occupied: The Origins and Future of Occupy Wall Street," *New Yorker*, November 21, 2011, https:// www.newyorker.com/magazine/2011/11/28/pre-occupied.

2. Michael Levitin, "The Triumph of Occupy Wall Street," *The Atlantic*, June 10, 2015, https://www.theatlantic.com/politics /archive/2015/06/the-triumph-of-occupy-wall-street/395408.

3. Levitin, "The Triumph of Occupy Wall Street."

4. Seth Godin, *Tribes: We Need You to Lead Us* (New York: Portfolio, 2008), 86.

5. "Montgomery Bus Boycott," History, last updated February 10,

2020, https://www.history.com/topics/black-history/montgomery
-bus-boycott.

6. "Martin Luther King Jr.," Biography, last updated January 23,
2020, https://www.biography.com/activist/martin-luther-king-jr.

7. "March on Washington for Jobs and Freedom," National Park
Service, last updated August 10, 2017, https://www.nps.gov
/articles/march-on-washington.htm, accessed March 5, 2020.

8. "Southern Christian Leadership Conference (SCLC)," The
Martin Luther King, Jr. Research and Education Institute,
Stanford University, accessed March 5, 2020, https://kinginstitute
.stanford.edu/encyclopedia/southern-christian-leadership
-conference-sclc.

9. "Martin Luther King Jr.," The Nobel Prize, accessed March 5,
2020, https://www.nobelprize.org/prizes/peace/1964/king
/biographical.

10. Chandler Foundation, "Prosperity," 51.

11. Fredreka Schouten, "Ad Spending Barrels Past $1 Billion Mark
As Mike Bloomberg Overwhelms Airwaves," CNN, February 28,
2020, https://www.cnn.com/2020/02/28/politics/2020-ad
-spending-1-billion/index.html.

12. Bill Allison and Mark Niquette, "Bloomberg Tops Half a Billion
Dollars in Campaign Advertising," Bloomberg, February 24,
2020, https://www.bloomberg.com/news/articles/2020–02–24
/bloomberg-tops-half-a-billion-dollars-in-campaign-advertising.

13. Zusha Elinson, "Mike Bloomberg's $620 Million Campaign Did
Really Well—in American Samoa," *Wall Street Journal*, March 6,
2020, https://www.wsj.com/articles/mike-bloombergs-620
-million-campaign-did-really-wellin-american-samoa
-11583538043.

14. James Truslow Adams, *The Epic of America* (1931, reprint, New
York: Routledge, 2017), 404, Kindle.

15. Martin Luther King Jr., "Beyond Vietnam," New York, NY, April 4,

1967, The Martin Luther King, Jr. Research and Education Institute, Stanford University, accessed March 10, 2020, https://kinginstitute. stanford.edu/king-papers/documents/beyond-vietnam.

16. Jakub Pigoń, ed., *The Children of Herodotus: Greek and Roman Historiography and Related Genres* (Newcastle: Cambridge Scholars, 2008), 135.

17. Dibin Samuel, "Wiliam [*sic*] Carey Played Significant Role in Abolishing Sati System," *Christianity Today*, December 4, 2009, http://www.christiantoday.co.in/article/wiliam.carey.played. significant.role.in.abolishing.sati.system/4906.htm.

18. Rodd Wagner and Gale Muller, *Power of 2: How to Make the Most of Your Partnerships at Work and in Life* (New York: Gallup Press, 2009), 8–10.

19. Wagner and Muller, 45.

CHAPTER 5: EXPERIENCE THE VALUE OF VALUES

1. Matthew 7:12 NLT.

2. Sahih Muslim, Book 1, Number 72, quoted in "Golden Rule in Islam," Islam.ru, February 26, 2013.

3. Talmud, Shabbat 3id, quoted in "The Universality of the Golden Rule in World Religions," http://www.teachingvalues .com/goldenrule.html.

4. Udana-Varga 5,1, quoted in "The Universality of the Golden Rule in World Religions.

5. Mahabharata 5,1517, quoted in "The Universality of the Golden Rule in World Religions.

6. Shayast-na-Shayast 13:29, quoted in "The Golden Rule Is Universal," Golden Rule Project, https://www.goldenruleproject .org/formulations.

7. Analects 15:23, quoted in "The Golden Rule Is Universal."

8. Epistle to the Son of the Wolf, quoted in "The Golden Rule Is Universal."

9. Sutrakritanga 1.11.33, quoted in "The Golden Rule Is Universal."

10. African proverb quoted in "The Golden Rule Is Universal."

11. Simon Sinek, *The Infinite Game* (New York: Portfolio/Penguin, 2019), 33–34.

12. Sinek, 37.

13. James Dobson, Commencement Address, Seattle Pacific University, June 1988.

14. "Well-Known Quotes by Millard Fuller," The Fuller Center for Housing, accessed June 16, 2020, https://fullercenter.org/quotes.

15. Bill Perkins, *Awaken the Leader Within: How the Wisdom of Jesus Can Unleash Your Potential* (Grand Rapids: Zondervan, 2000), 35–36.

16. Ishika Chawla, "CDC Releases Preliminary Findings on Palo Alto Suicide Clusters," *Stanford Daily*, July 21, 2016, https://www.stanforddaily.com/2016/07/21/cdc-releases-preliminary-findings-on-palo-alto-suicide-clusters.

17. "Social and Emotional Skills: Well-being, Connectedness, and Success," OECD, accessed March 16, 2020, https://www.oecd.org/education/school/UPDATED%20Social%20and%20Emotional%20Skills%20-%20Well-being,%20connectedness%20and%20success.pdf%20(website).pdf.

18. Stephen R. Covey, A. Roger Merrill, and Rebecca R. Merrill, *First Things First: To Live, to Love, to Learn, to Leave a Legacy* (New York: Simon & Schuster, 1994) 12.

19. Diane Kalen-Sukra, *Save Your City: How Toxic Culture Kills Community and What to Do About It* (Victoria, BC, Canada: Municipal World, 2019), 94.

20. Sarah Pulliam Bailey, "A Megachurch Has Helped Test Nearly 1,000 People for Coronavirus in Two Days," *Washington Post*, March 19, 2020, https://www.washingtonpost.com/religion/2020/03/19/megachurch-has-nearly-1000-people-tested-coronavirus-two-days.

21. Bailey, "A Megachurch Has Helped Test Nearly 1,000 People for Coronavirus in Two Days," https://www.washingtonpost.com /religion/2020/03/19/megachurch-has-nearly-1000-people-tested -coronavirus-two-days.

22. U.S. Senate, Committee on Governmental Affairs, Permanent Subcommittee on Investigations, *The Role of the Board of Directors in Enron's Collapse: Hearing Before the Permanent Subcommittee of Investigations of the Committee on Governmental Affairs, United States Senate, One Hundred Seventh Congress, Second Session, May 7, 2002* (Washington, DC: Government Printing Office, 2002), 293, https://books.google.com/books?id=NcM1AAAAI AAJ&pg=PA293&lpg=PA293&dq=%22Communication+–+" We+have+an+obligation+to+communicate.+Here,+we+take+the +time+to+talk+with+one+another. . .and+to+listen.+We+believe +that+information+is+meant+to+move,+and+that+information +moves+people."&source=bl&ots=JOjEub12YO&sig=ACfU3U 0ZiPdn6BRis3AmVejAd-OakJ70fA&hl=en&sa=X&ved=2ahUK EwjQhaOEl7jnAhUhTd8KHbc3BJQQ6AEwCXoECAcQAQ #v=onepage&q=%22Communication%20–%20"We%20have %20an%20obligation%20to%20communicate.%20Here%2C %20we%20take%20the%20time%20to%20talk%20with%20one %20another. . .and%20to%20listen.%20We%20believe%20that %20information%20is%20meant%20to%20move%2C%20and %20that%20information%20moves%20people."&f=false.

23. Troy Segal, "Enron Scandal: The Fall of a Wall Street Darling," Investopedia, last updated May 29, 2019 , https://www.investopedia .com/updates/enron-scandal-summary.

24. "Bantrab," Financial Advisory.com, accessed February 10, 2020, https://guatemala.financialadvisory.com/about/bantrab/.

25. Juan Pablo de León, interview by Carolina Donis-Lockwood, December 7, 2019.

26. Richard Barrett, "The Importance of Values in Building a High

Performance Culture," Barrett Values Centre, February 2010, 5, https://fliphtml5.com/uono/ahbn.

27. *Evaluation Report for Lead Today: Ghana*, OneHope (Pompano Beach, FL: OneHope, 2016), 2.

28. "Summary Report: EQUIP Leadership Program, Ghana Pilot Validation," OneHope, July 2, 2015, 1.

CHAPTER 6: TRANSFORMATION HAPPENS ONE TABLE AT A TIME

1. Sheryl Sandberg with Nell Scovell, *Lean In: Women, Work, and the Will to Lead* (New York: Alfred A. Knopf, 2013)149 of 173, Kindle.

2. Nicholas A. Christakis and James H. Fowler, *Connected: The Surprising Power of Our Social Networks and How They Shape Our Lives—How Your Friends' Friends' Friends Affect Everything You Feel, Think, and Do* (New York: Little, Brown Spark, 2009), 87 of 5128, Kindle.

3. James Clear, *Atomic Habits: Tiny Changes, Remarkable Results—An Easy and Proven Way to Build Good Habits and Break Bad Ones* (New York: Avery, 2018), 144–147.

4. Clear, 36–37.

5. Clear, 30–31, 36.

CHAPTER 7: WHAT GETS DONE GETS MEASURED

1. Tom Rath, *Life's Greatest Question: Discover How You Contribute to the World* (Arlington, VA: Silicon Guild, 2020), 9 of 109, Kindle.

2. Quoted in Rath, *Life's Greatest Question*, 12 of 109, Kindle.

3. Rath, 28 of 109, Kindle.

4. John Doerr, *Measure What Matters: How Google, Bono, and the Gates Foundation Rock the World with OKRs* (New York: Portfolio/Penguin, 2018), 3.

5. "The 100 Largest Companies in the World by Market Value in 2019," *Statista*, accessed April 17, 2020 https://www.statista.com/statistics/263264/top-companies-in-the-world-by-market-value.

6. Brand Finance, "BrandFinance Global 500 (100) 2020," Ranking t he Brands, accessed April 17, 2020, https://www.rankingthebrands.com/The-Brand-Rankings.aspx?rankingID=83&year=1289.

7. Ng Han Guan, "The 100 Best Companies to Work For," Fortune, accessed April 17, 2020, https://fortune.com/best-companies/2017/google.

8. Doerr, 6 of 306, Kindle.

9. Jim Collins, "The Flywheel Effect," Jim Collins, accessed April 17. 2020, https://www.jimcollins.com/concepts/the-flywheel.html.

10. Quoted in Doerr, 177 of 306, Kindle.

11. Quoted in Doerr, 181 of 306, Kindle.

12. Yogi Berra, *The Yogi Book: "I Really Didn't Say Everything I Said!"* (New York: Workman, 2010), 502 of 819, Kindle.

13. Charles D. Lanier, "Two Giants of the Electric Age," *Review of Reviews*, July 1893, 44, https://books.google.com/books?id=mbsrAQAAIAAJ&pg=PA1&lpg=PA1&dq=%22Two+Giants+of+the+Electric+Age%22+Review+of+Reviews+July+1893&source=bl&ots=sSfYFCJKJv&sig=ACfU3U0q-1jSx1ZBMTbTEYmoDHNE86WDdA&hl=en&sa=X&ved=2ahUKEwjMn4uQg4nqAhXUTDABHarwAPwQ6AEwAHoECAUQAQ#v=onepage&q&f=false.

14. Peter F. Drucker, *The Effective Executive* (1967, reprint, New York: HarperCollins, 2002), 33 of 165, Kindle.

15. Dave Smith, comp, *The Quotable Walt Disney* (Los Angeles: Disney Editions, 2001), 246 of 263, Kindle.

16. Marianne Schnall, "An Interview with Maya Angelou," *Psychology Today*, February 17, 2009, https://www.psychologytoday.com/us/blog/the-guest-room/200902/interview-maya-angelou.

17. Malcolm Gladwell, *The Tipping Point: How Little Things Can Make*

a Big Difference (New York: Little, Brown and Company, 2002), 11 of 259, Kindle.

18. "Minority Rules: Scientists Discover Tipping Point for the Spread of Ideas," Rensselaer Polytechnic Institute, July 25, 2011, https://news.rpi.edu/luwakkey/2902.

19. John Dewey, *How We Think* (Boston: D. D. Heath & Co., 1910), 78.

20. "Woman Behind Blessings in a Backpack Honored," Blessings in a Backpack, October 2, 2018, https://www.blessingsinabackpack.org/missy-hammerstrom-blessingsday18.

21. "Gifts to Our Community: Blessings in a Backpack," Today's Woman, December 9, 2019, https://www.todayswomannow.com/2019/12/gifts-to-our-community-blessings-in-a-backpack.html.

CHAPTER 8: LET'S KEEP TALKING

1. Judy Wilson, "The Horror of Marjory Stoneman Douglas Inspired School Administrator to Introduce Students to Be Strong Resilience Program," New Pelican, February 14, 2020, https://www.newpelican.com/articles/the-horror-of-marjory-stoneman-douglas-inspired-school-administrator-to-introduce-students-to-be-strong-resilience-program.

2. Roy Moore, interview by author, April 3, 2020.

3. Peter Drucker, *Managing in Turbulent Times* (New York: Routledge, 1993), x.

4. Shane J. Lopez, *Making Hope Happen: Create the Future You Want for Yourself and Others* (New York: Atria, 2013), 71 of 200, Kindle.

5. Lopez, 71–72 of 200, Kindle.

6. Casey Gwinn and Chan Hellman, *Hope Rising: How the Science of Hope Can Change Your Life* (New York: Morgan James, 2018), xvi.

7. Gwinn and Hellman, 9.

8. For information on these studies, see Katie Hanson, "What Exactly Is Hope and How Can You Measure It?" Positive Psychology, October 24, 2009, http://positivepsychology.org.uk /hope-theory-snyder-adult-scale.

9. Vanessa Boris, "What Makes Storytelling So Effective for Learning?" Harvard Business Publishing, December 20, 2017, https://www.harvardbusiness.org/what-makes -storytelling-so-effective-for-learning.

10. Kari Berger, "The Truth in Story: An Interview with Merna Hecht," Context Institute, Fall 1989, https://www.context.org /iclib/ic23/hecht.

11. Christopher Ross, "Stories Stick and There Is the Science to Prove It," Fipp, August 15, 2016, https://www.fipp.com/news /features/stories-stick-and-there-is-the-science-to-prove-it.

12. "50 Best Quotes for Storytelling," The Storyteller Agency, accessed April 1, 2020, http://thestorytelleragency.com /goodreads/50-best-quotes-for-storytelling.

CHAPTER 9: IT'S YOUR TURN TO CHANGE YOUR WORLD

1. "Crisis, Mission, and Vision," Ēma South Florida, accessed April 7, 2020, https://www.emasouthflorida.org/who-we-are/crisis -vision-and-mission.

2. Becky Bursell, interview by author, April 23, 2020.

About the Authors

John C. Maxwell

John C. Maxwell is a #1 *New York Times* bestselling author, speaker, coach, and leader who has sold more than 33 million books in fifty languages. He has been called the #1 leader in business and the most influential leadership expert in the world. His organizations—the John Maxwell Company, the John Maxwell Team, EQUIP, and the John Maxwell Leadership Foundation—have translated his teachings into seventy languages and used them to train millions of leaders from every country in the world. A recipient of the Horatio Alger Award and the Mother Teresa Prize for Global Peace and Leadership from the Luminary Leadership Network, Dr. Maxwell influences Fortune 500 CEOs, the presidents of nations, and entrepreneurs worldwide. For more information about him visit JohnMaxwell.com.

Rob Hoskins

Called "a leader of leaders" by John Maxwell, Rob has committed his life to building young leaders and serving great leaders. He does this by overseeing startups, spearheading sustainable local & global transformation initiatives, or advising NGOs and higher education institutions. Rob often guides the modernization of existing enterprises or successful transitions. He also consults for corporations to help revitalize their mission and vision, then scale for growth.

Rob is also known for relentlessly applying research, data, and metrics to accelerate results and has pioneered an innovative process to measure outcomes rather than outputs. He has been President of OneHope, Inc. since 2004. Learn more at RobHoskins.net.